U.S. Department of Transportation
Federal Aviation Administration

FAA-S-ACS-25
Includes FAA-G-ACS-2

Airman Certification Standards

Flight Instructor

Airplane

T0015061

AVIATION SUPPLIES & ACADEMICS, INC.
NEWCASTLE, WASHINGTON

Flight Instructor Airplane Airman Certification Standards

Aviation Supplies & Academics, Inc.
7005 132nd Place SE
Newcastle, Washington 98059
asa@asa2fly.com | 425-235-1500 | asa2fly.com

Visit asa2fly.com/acsupdates for FAA revisions affecting this title.

None of the material in this book supersedes any operational documents or procedures issued by the Federal Aviation Administration.

ASA-ACS-25
ISBN 978-1-64425-456-1

Additional formats available:
eBook EPUB   ISBN 978-1-64425-457-8
eBook PDF   ISBN 978-1-64425-458-5

Printed in the United States of America

2028 2027 2026 2025 2024   9 8 7 6 5 4 3 2 1

Contents

U.S. Department
of Transportation

**Federal Aviation
Administration**

Flight Instructor for Airplane Category
Airman Certification Standards

November 2023

Flight Standards Service
Washington, DC 20591

Foreword

The U.S. Department of Transportation, Federal Aviation Administration (FAA), Office of Safety Standards, Regulatory Support Division, Airman Testing Standards Branch, has published the Flight Instructor for Airplane Category Airman Certification Standards (ACS) to communicate the aeronautical knowledge, risk management, and flight proficiency standards for the Flight Instructor Certificate in the airplane category.

This ACS is available for download, in PDF format, from www.faa.gov.

Comments regarding this ACS may be emailed to acsptsinquiries@faa.gov.

Material in FAA-S-ACS-25 supersedes FAA-S-8081-6D, Flight Instructor Practical Test Standards for Airplane, dated June 2012.

The FAA created FAA-G-ACS-2, Airman Certification Standards Companion Guide for Pilots, to provide guidance considered relevant and useful to the community. The number of appendices in the ACS was reduced and much of the non-regulatory material was moved to the Airman Certification Standards Companion Guide for Pilots. Applicants, instructors, and evaluators should consult this companion guide to familiarize themselves with ACS procedures. FAA-G-ACS-2 is available for download, in PDF format, from www.faa.gov.

Revision History

Document #	Description	Date
FAA-S-8081-6D	Flight Instructor Practical Test Standards for Airplane (with Changes 1–6)	June 2012
FAA-S-ACS-25	Flight Instructor for Airplane Category Airman Certification Standards	November 2023

Table of Contents

Introduction

Airman Certification Standards Concept

The goal of the airman certification process is to ensure the applicant possesses the knowledge, ability to manage risks, and skill consistent with the privileges of the certificate or rating being exercised, in order to act as pilot-in-command (PIC).

Safe operations in today's National Airspace System (NAS) require the integration of aeronautical knowledge, risk management, and flight proficiency standards. To accomplish these goals, the FAA drew upon the expertise of organizations and individuals across the aviation and training community to develop the ACS. The ACS integrates the elements of knowledge, risk management, and skill required for each airman certificate or rating. It thus forms a more comprehensive standard for what an applicant must know, consider, and do to demonstrate proficiency to pass the tests required for issuance of the applicable airman certificate or rating.

Area of Operation I. Fundamentals of Instructing

Note: *The evaluator must select Task E, Task F, and at least one other Task for initial flight instructor applicants. During a practical test for an added flight instructor rating or flight instructor reinstatement, the evaluator has discretion to evaluate the applicant on Fundamentals of Instructing.*

Task A. Effects of Human Behavior and Communication on the Learning Process

References: *FAA-H-8083-2, FAA-H-8083-9, FAA-H-8083-25*

Objective: To determine the applicant understands human behavior and effective communication, can apply that knowledge, manage associated risks, demonstrate appropriate skills, and provide effective instruction.

Knowledge:	The applicant understands and explains:
FI.I.A.K1	Elements of human behavior, including:
FI.I.A.K1a	a. Definitions of human behavior
FI.I.A.K1b	b. Instructor and learner relationship
FI.I.A.K1c	c. Motivation
FI.I.A.K1d	d. Human needs
FI.I.A.K1e	e. Defense mechanisms
FI.I.A.K2	Learner emotional reactions, including:
FI.I.A.K2a	a. Anxiety and stress
FI.I.A.K2b	b. Impatience
FI.I.A.K2c	c. Worry or lack of interest
FI.I.A.K2d	d. Physical discomfort, illness, fatigue, and dehydration
FI.I.A.K2e	e. Apathy due to inadequate instruction
FI.I.A.K3	Teaching the adult learner.
FI.I.A.K4	Effective communication, including:
FI.I.A.K4a	a. Basic elements of communication
FI.I.A.K4b	b. Barriers to effective communication
FI.I.A.K4c	c. Developing communication skills

Risk Management:	The applicant is able to identify, assess, and mitigate risk associated with:
FI.I.A.R1	Recognizing and accommodating human behavior.
FI.I.A.R2	Barriers to communication.

Skills:	The applicant exhibits the skill to:
FI.I.A.S1	Give examples of how human behavior affects motivation and learning.
FI.I.A.S2	Describe what the instructor can do to deal with:
FI.I.A.S2a	a. Serious abnormal emotional behavior
FI.I.A.S2b	b. Defense mechanisms
FI.I.A.S3	Use effective communication in ground and flight instruction.

Task B. Learning Process

References: *FAA-H-8083-2, FAA-H-8083-9, FAA-H-8083-25*

Objective: To determine the applicant understands the learning process, can apply that knowledge, manage associated risks, demonstrate appropriate skills, and provide effective instruction.

Knowledge:	The applicant understands and explains:
FI.I.B.K1	Definitions of learning.
FI.I.B.K2	Learning theory as it applies to ground and flight instruction, including:
FI.I.B.K2a	a. Behaviorism
FI.I.B.K2b	b. Cognitive Theory
FI.I.B.K3	Perceptions and insight.
FI.I.B.K4	Acquiring knowledge.
FI.I.B.K5	Laws of learning.
FI.I.B.K6	Domains of learning, including:
FI.I.B.K6a	a. Cognitive
FI.I.B.K6b	b. Affective
FI.I.B.K6c	c. Psychomotor
FI.I.B.K7	Characteristics of learning.
FI.I.B.K8	Scenario-based training (SBT).
FI.I.B.K9	Acquiring skill knowledge, including:
FI.I.B.K9a	a. Stages
FI.I.B.K9b	b. Knowledge of results
FI.I.B.K9c	c. How to develop skills
FI.I.B.K9d	d. Learning plateaus
FI.I.B.K10	Types of practice.
FI.I.B.K11	Evaluation versus critique.
FI.I.B.K12	Distractions, interruptions, fixation, and inattention.
FI.I.B.K13	Errors.
FI.I.B.K14	Memory, including:
FI.I.B.K14a	a. Sensory
FI.I.B.K14b	b. Short-Term Memory (STM) and Long-Term Memory (LTM)
FI.I.B.K14c	c. How usage affects memory
FI.I.B.K14d	d. Forgetting
FI.I.B.K15	Retention of learning.
FI.I.B.K16	Transfer of learning.

Risk Management:	The applicant is able to identify, assess, and mitigate risk associated with:
FI.I.B.R1	Inadequate or incomplete instruction.

FI.I.B.R2	Lack of learner motivation.
FI.I.B.R3	Recognizing and correcting learner errors.

Skills:	The applicant exhibits the skill to:
FI.I.B.S1	Apply educational theories to ground and flight instruction.
FI.I.B.S2	Recognize and correct conditions that undermine the learning process.
FI.I.B.S3	Plan for and use techniques, including realistic distractions that teach flight students how to manage a workload.

Task C. Course Development, Lesson Plans, and Classroom Training Techniques

References: FAA-H-8083-2, FAA-H-8083-9, FAA-H-8083-25

Objective: To determine the applicant understands the teaching process, can apply that knowledge, manage associated risks, demonstrate appropriate skills, and provide effective instruction.

Knowledge:	The applicant understands and explains:
FI.I.C.K1	Teaching, including:
FI.I.C.K1a	a. Process
FI.I.C.K1b	b. Essential skills
FI.I.C.K2	Course of training.
FI.I.C.K3	Preparation of a lesson, including:
FI.I.C.K3a	a. Training objectives and completion standards
FI.I.C.K3b	b. Performance-based objectives
FI.I.C.K3c	c. Importance of Airman Certification Standards (ACS) in aviation training curricula
FI.I.C.K3d	d. Decision-based objectives
FI.I.C.K4	Organization of material.
FI.I.C.K5	Training delivery methods, including:
FI.I.C.K5a	a. Lecture
FI.I.C.K5b	b. Discussion
FI.I.C.K5c	c. Guided discussion
FI.I.C.K5d	d. Cooperative or group learning
FI.I.C.K5e	e. Demonstration-performance
FI.I.C.K5f	f. Drill and practice
FI.I.C.K6	Electronic learning (e-Learning).
FI.I.C.K7	Instructional aids and training technologies, including:
FI.I.C.K7a	a. Characteristics of effective instructional aids
FI.I.C.K7b	b. Reasons for use
FI.I.C.K7c	c. Guidelines for use
FI.I.C.K7d	d. Types

FI.I.C.K8	Integrated flight instruction.
FI.I.C.K9	Problem-based instruction.
FI.I.C.K10	Planning instructional activity, including:
FI.I.C.K10a	a. Blocks of learning
FI.I.C.K10b	b. Training syllabus
FI.I.C.K10c	c. Lesson plans

Risk Management: The applicant is able to identify, assess, and mitigate risk associated with:

| FI.I.C.R1 | Selection of teaching method. |

Skills: The applicant exhibits the skill to:

FI.I.C.S1	Prepare an instructional lesson plan using teaching methods and materials appropriate for Task and learner characteristics, including:
FI.I.C.S1a	a. Aeronautical knowledge ground lesson applicable for a classroom
FI.I.C.S1b	b. Maneuver introduction and ground lesson

Task D. Student Evaluation, Assessment, and Testing

References: FAA-H-8083-2, FAA-H-8083-9, FAA-H-8083-25

Objective: To determine the applicant understands evaluation and testing, can apply that knowledge, manage associated risks, demonstrate appropriate skills, and provide effective instruction.

Knowledge: The applicant understands and explains:

FI.I.D.K1	Purpose and characteristics of effective assessment.
FI.I.D.K2	Traditional assessments.
FI.I.D.K3	Authentic assessments, including:
FI.I.D.K3a	a. Learner-centered assessment
FI.I.D.K3b	b. Maneuver or procedure grades
FI.I.D.K3c	c. Assessing risk management skills
FI.I.D.K4	Choosing an effective assessment method.
FI.I.D.K5	Purposes and types of critiques.
FI.I.D.K6	Oral assessment, including:
FI.I.D.K6a	a. Characteristics of effective questions
FI.I.D.K6b	b. Types of questions to avoid
FI.I.D.K6c	c. Answering learner questions
FI.I.D.K7	Assessment of piloting ability.

Risk Management: The applicant is able to identify, assess, and mitigate risk associated with:

| FI.I.D.R1 | Delivering an assessment. |

Skills: The applicant exhibits the skill to:

FI.I.D.S1 Use appropriate methods and techniques to assess learner performance in ground or flight training.

Task E. Elements of Effective Teaching in a Professional Environment

References: *FAA-H-8083-2, FAA-H-8083-9, FAA-H-8083-25*

Objective: To determine the applicant understands effects of instructor behavior on effective teaching, can apply that knowledge, manage associated risks, demonstrate appropriate skills, and provide effective instruction.

Knowledge: The applicant demonstrates understanding of:

FI.I.E.K1 Aviation instructor responsibilities, including:

FI.I.E.K1a a. Helping learners

FI.I.E.K1b b. Providing adequate instruction

FI.I.E.K1c c. Training to established standards of performance

FI.I.E.K1d d. Emphasizing the positive

FI.I.E.K1e e. Minimizing learner frustrations

FI.I.E.K2 Flight instructor responsibilities, including supervision and surveillance during training.

FI.I.E.K3 Flight instructor qualifications and professionalism.

FI.I.E.K4 Professional development.

FI.I.E.K5 Instructor ethics and conduct.

Risk Management: The applicant is able to identify, assess, and mitigate risk associated with:

FI.I.E.R1 Fulfilling instructor responsibilities.

FI.I.E.R2 Exhibiting professionalism.

Skills: The applicant exhibits the skill to:

FI.I.E.S1 Deliver ground or flight instruction on an evaluator-assigned Task in a manner consistent with instructor responsibilities and professional characteristics as stated in K1 through K5.

Task F. Elements of Effective Teaching that Include Risk Management and Accident Prevention

References: *FAA-H-8083-2, FAA-H-8083-9, FAA-H-8083-25*

Objective: To determine the applicant understands teaching practical risk management, can apply that knowledge, manage associated risks, demonstrate appropriate skills, and provide effective instruction.

Knowledge: The applicant understands and explains:

FI.I.F.K1 Teaching risk identification, assessment, and mitigation.

FI.I.F.K2 Teaching risk management tools, including:

FI.I.F.K2a a. Pilot/Aircraft/enVironment/External Pressures (PAVE) checklist

FI.I.F.K2b	b. Flight Risk Assessment Tools (FRATs)
FI.I.F.K3	When and how to introduce risk management.
FI.I.F.K4	Risk management teaching techniques by phase of instruction.
FI.I.F.K5	Managing risk during flight instruction, including:
FI.I.F.K5a	a. Common flight instruction risks
FI.I.F.K5b	b. Best practices
FI.I.F.K5c	c. Special considerations while teaching takeoffs and landings
FI.I.F.K6	Aeronautical Decision-Making (ADM) to include using Crew Resource Management (CRM) or Single- Pilot Resource Management (SRM), as appropriate.

Risk Management: The applicant is able to identify, assess, and mitigate risk associated with:

FI.I.F.R1	Hazards associated with providing flight instruction.
FI.I.F.R2	Obstacles to maintaining situational awareness during flight instruction.
FI.I.F.R3	Recognizing and managing hazards arising from human behavior, including hazardous attitudes.

Skills: The applicant exhibits the skill to:

FI.I.F.S1	Use scenario-based training (SBT) to demonstrate, teach, and assess risk management and Aeronautical Decision-Making (ADM) skills in the context of a Task specified by the evaluator.
FI.I.F.S2	Identify, assess, and mitigate risks commonly associated with flight instruction by maintaining:
FI.I.F.S2a	a. Awareness and oversight of the learner's actions, with timely and appropriate supervision, intervention, or mitigation as needed
FI.I.F.S2b	b. Awareness of the learner's cognitive/physiological state, with timely action to mitigate anxiety, fatigue, or other obstruction to learning
FI.I.F.S2c	c. Overall situational awareness of the aircraft's dynamic state, its position in space, and vigilance for unexpected events or changing circumstances that occur in the environment
FI.I.F.S3	Model and teach safety practices, including maintaining:
FI.I.F.S3a	a. Collision avoidance while simultaneously providing instruction
FI.I.F.S3b	b. Avoidance of unnecessary distractions
FI.I.F.S3c	c. Coordinated flight
FI.I.F.S3d	d. Awareness of who is manipulating controls through positive exchange of flight controls
FI.I.F.S3e	e. Continuous awareness of the aircraft's dynamic state and position in the NAS

Area of Operation II. Technical Subject Areas

Note: *The evaluator must select Tasks C, K, and at least one other Task from this Area of Operation. The evaluator must also select Task P for multiengine applicants.*

Task A. Human Factors

References: *AIM; FAA-H-8083-2, FAA-H-8083-3, FAA-H-8083-9, FAA-H-8083-25*

Objective: To determine the applicant understands personal health, flight physiology, aeromedical and human factors, can apply that knowledge, manage associated risks, demonstrate appropriate skills, and provide effective instruction.

Knowledge:	The applicant demonstrates instructional knowledge by describing and explaining:
AI.II.A.K1	Symptoms, recognition, causes, effects, and corrective actions associated with aeromedical and physiological issues, including:
AI.II.A.K1a	a. Hypoxia
AI.II.A.K1b	b. Hyperventilation
AI.II.A.K1c	c. Middle ear and sinus problems
AI.II.A.K1d	d. Spatial disorientation
AI.II.A.K1e	e. Motion sickness
AI.II.A.K1f	f. Carbon monoxide poisoning
AI.II.A.K1g	g. Stress
AI.II.A.K1h	h. Fatigue
AI.II.A.K1i	i. Dehydration and nutrition
AI.II.A.K1j	j. Hypothermia
AI.II.A.K1k	k. Optical illusions
AI.II.A.K1l	l. Dissolved nitrogen in the bloodstream after scuba dives
AI.II.A.K2	Regulations regarding use of alcohol and drugs.
AI.II.A.K3	Effects of alcohol, drugs, and over-the-counter medications.
AI.II.A.K4	Aeronautical Decision-Making (ADM) to include using Crew Resource Management (CRM) or Single-Pilot Resource Management (SRM), as appropriate.

Risk Management:	The applicant explains and teaches how to identify and manage risk associated with:
AI.II.A.R1	Aeromedical and physiological issues.
AI.II.A.R2	Hazardous attitudes.
AI.II.A.R3	Distractions, task prioritization, loss of situational awareness, or disorientation.
AI.II.A.R4	Confirmation and expectation bias.

Skills:	The applicant demonstrates and simultaneously explains how to:
AI.II.A.S1	Associate the symptoms and effects for at least three of the conditions listed in K1a through K1l with the cause(s) and corrective action(s).
AI.II.A.S2	Perform self-assessment, including fitness for flight and personal minimums, for actual flight or a scenario given by the evaluator.

Task B. Visual Scanning and Collision Avoidance

References: *AC 90-48; AIM; FAA-H-8083-2, FAA-H-8083-3, FAA-H-8083-9, FAA-H-8083-25*

Objective: To determine the applicant understands visual scanning and collision avoidance, can apply that knowledge, manage associated risks, demonstrate pilot-in-command skills, and provide effective instruction.

Knowledge:	The applicant demonstrates instructional knowledge by describing and explaining:
AI.II.B.K1	Environmental conditions that degrade vision.
AI.II.B.K2	Vestibular and visual illusions.
AI.II.B.K3	"See and Avoid" responsibilities.
AI.II.B.K4	Visual scanning procedure and the importance of peripheral vision.
AI.II.B.K5	Aircraft blind spots and clearing procedures.
AI.II.B.K6	Visual cues of an impending mid-air collision.
AI.II.B.K7	Situations that create the greatest collision risk.
AI.II.B.K8	Division of attention inside and outside the aircraft.

Risk Management:	The applicant explains and teaches how to identify and manage risk associated with:
AI.II.B.R1	Distractions to visual scanning.
AI.II.B.R2	Relaxed intermediate focal distance.
AI.II.B.R3	High volume operational environments.
AI.II.B.R4	Collision reaction time.
AI.II.B.R5	Use of a safety pilot.

Skills:	The applicant demonstrates and simultaneously explains how to:
AI.II.B.S1	Effectively scan using short regularly spaced eye movements.
AI.II.B.S2	Scan around physical obstructions.
AI.II.B.S3	Use appropriate visual scanning techniques.
AI.II.B.S4	Use electronic traffic alert systems, if available.

Task C. Runway Incursion Avoidance

References: *AC 91-73; AIM; Chart Supplements; FAA-H-8083-2, FAA-H-8083-3, FAA-H-8083-9, FAA-H-8083-25*

Objective: To determine the applicant understands runway incursion avoidance, can apply that knowledge, manage associated risks, demonstrate appropriate skills, and provide effective instruction.

Knowledge:	The applicant demonstrates instructional knowledge by describing and explaining:
AI.II.C.K1	Runway incursion definition.
AI.II.C.K2	Taxi instructions/clearances.
AI.II.C.K3	The importance of recording taxi instructions and reviewing taxi routes on the airport diagram.

AI.II.C.K4	Airport markings, signs, and lights including the importance of hold lines associated with runways.
AI.II.C.K5	Appropriate flight deck activities during taxiing, including taxi route planning, briefing the location of Hot Spots, communicating and coordinating with ATC.
AI.II.C.K6	Communication and operational procedures at uncontrolled airports.

Risk Management: The applicant explains and teaches how to identify and manage risk associated with:

AI.II.C.R1	Distractions, task prioritization, loss of situational awareness, or disorientation.
AI.II.C.R2	Confirmation or expectation bias as related to taxi instructions.
AI.II.C.R3	Entering or crossing runways.
AI.II.C.R4	Night taxi operations.
AI.II.C.R5	Low visibility taxi operations.
AI.II.C.R6	Runway incursion after landing.
AI.II.C.R7	Operating on taxiways between parallel runways.

Skills: The applicant demonstrates how to:

| AI.II.C.S1 | Deliver instruction on the elements and techniques for runway incursion avoidance. |

Task D. Principles of Flight

References: FAA-H-8083-2, FAA-H-8083-3, FAA-H-8083-9, FAA-H-8083-23, FAA-H-8083-25; POH/AFM

Objective: To determine the applicant understands aerodynamics appropriate to the desired instructor certificate, can apply that knowledge, manage associated risks, demonstrate appropriate skills, and provide effective instruction.

Knowledge: The applicant demonstrates instructional knowledge by describing and explaining:

AI.II.D.K1	Airfoil design characteristics.
AI.II.D.K2	Airplane stability, maneuverability and controllability.
AI.II.D.K3	Turning tendency (e.g., torque, p-factor, spiraling slipstream, and gyroscopic precession).
AI.II.D.K4	Forces acting on an airplane.
AI.II.D.K5	Load factors in airplane design.
AI.II.D.K6	Wingtip vortices and appropriate precautions.

Risk Management: The applicant explains and teaches how to identify and manage risk associated with:

| AI.II.D.R1 | The basic aerodynamic principles of flight. |

Skills: The applicant demonstrates how to:

| AI.II.D.S1 | Deliver instruction on principles of flight, including at least three of the elements listed in K1 through K6. |

Task E. Aircraft Flight Controls and Operation of Systems

References: *FAA-H-8083-2, FAA-H-8083-3, FAA-H-8083-9, FAA-H-8083-23, FAA-H-8083-25; POH/AFM*

Objective: To determine the applicant understands flight controls and systems on the airplane provided for the flight test, can apply that knowledge, manage associated risks, demonstrate appropriate skills, and provide effective instruction.

Note: *If K1 is selected, the evaluator must assess the applicant's knowledge of all sub-elements.*

Knowledge:	The applicant demonstrates instructional knowledge by describing and explaining:
AI.II.E.K1	Airplane systems, including:
AI.II.E.K1a	a. Primary flight controls
AI.II.E.K1b	b. Secondary flight controls
AI.II.E.K1c	c. Powerplant and propeller
AI.II.E.K1d	d. Landing gear
AI.II.E.K1e	e. Fuel, oil, and hydraulic
AI.II.E.K1f	f. Electrical
AI.II.E.K1g	g. Avionics
AI.II.E.K1h	h. Pitot-static, vacuum/pressure, and associated flight instruments
AI.II.E.K1i	i. Environmental
AI.II.E.K1j	j. Deicing and anti-icing
AI.II.E.K1k	k. Water rudders (ASES, AMES)
AI.II.E.K1l	l. Oxygen system
AI.II.E.K2	Indications of and procedures for managing system abnormalities or failures.

Risk Management:	The applicant explains and teaches how to identify and manage risk associated with:
AI.II.E.R1	Detection of system malfunctions or failures.
AI.II.E.R2	Management of a system failure.
AI.II.E.R3	Monitoring and management of automated systems.
AI.II.E.R4	Providing instruction in unfamiliar aircraft or operating with unfamiliar flight display systems and avionics.

Skills:	The applicant demonstrates and simultaneously explains how to:
AI.II.E.S1	Operate at least three of the systems listed in K1a through K1l appropriately.

Task F. Performance and Limitations

References: *FAA-H-8083-1, FAA-H-8083-2, FAA-H-8083-3, FAA-H-8083-9, FAA-H-8083-25; POH/AFM*

Objective: To determine the applicant understands aircraft performance and limitations, can apply that knowledge, manage associated risks, demonstrate appropriate skills, and provide effective instruction.

Knowledge:	The applicant demonstrates instructional knowledge by describing and explaining:

AI.II.F.K1	Elements related to performance and limitations by explaining the use of charts, tables, and data to determine performance.
AI.II.F.K2	Factors affecting performance, including:
AI.II.F.K2a	a. Atmospheric conditions
AI.II.F.K2b	b. Pilot technique
AI.II.F.K2c	c. Airplane configuration
AI.II.F.K2d	d. Airport environment
AI.II.F.K2e	e. Loading and weight and balance
AI.II.F.K3	Weight and balance terms, including: basic empty weight, maximum gross weight, arm, moment, reference datum, center of gravity (CG) and CG limits, and useful load.
AI.II.F.K4	Methods for computing CG.
AI.II.F.K5	Aerodynamics.

Risk Management:	The applicant explains and teaches how to identify and manage risk associated with:
AI.II.F.R1	Use of performance charts, tables, and data.
AI.II.F.R2	Airplane limitations.
AI.II.F.R3	Possible differences between calculated performance and actual performance.
AI.II.F.R4	Exceeding weight limits.
AI.II.F.R5	Operating outside of CG limits.
AI.II.F.R6	Shifting, adding, and removing weight.

Skills:	The applicant demonstrates and simultaneously explains how to:
AI.II.F.S1	Use the appropriate airplane performance charts, tables, and data.
AI.II.F.S2	Compute the weight and balance, correct out-of-center of gravity loading errors and determine if the weight and balance remains within limits during all phases of flight.

Task G. National Airspace System

References:	14 CFR parts 71, 91, 93; AIM; FAA-H-8083-2, FAA-H-8083-3, FAA-H-8083-9, FAA-H-8083-25; VFR Navigation Charts
Objective:	To determine the applicant understands the National Airspace System, can apply that knowledge, manage associated risks, demonstrate appropriate skills, and provide effective instruction.

Knowledge:	The applicant demonstrates instructional knowledge by describing and explaining:
AI.II.G.K1	Airspace classes and associated requirements and limitations.
AI.II.G.K2	Chart symbols.
AI.II.G.K3	Special use airspace (SUA), special flight rules areas (SFRA), temporary flight restrictions (TFR), and other airspace areas.
AI.II.G.K4	Currency of publications.
AI.II.G.K5	Special visual flight rules (VFR) requirements.

Risk Management: The applicant explains and teaches how to identify and manage risk associated with:

AI.II.G.R1	Various classes and types of airspace.

Skills: The applicant demonstrates and simultaneously explains how to:

AI.II.G.S1	Identify and comply with the requirements for basic VFR weather minimums and flying in particular classes of airspace.
AI.II.G.S2	Correctly identify airspace and operate in accordance with associated communication and equipment requirements.
AI.II.G.S3	Identify the requirements for operating in SUA or within a TFR. Identify and comply with special air traffic rules (SATR) and SFRA operations, if applicable.

Task H. Navigation Systems and Radar Services

References: AC 91-78; AIM; FAA-H-8083-2, FAA-H-8083-3, FAA-H-8083-9, FAA-H-8083-25

Objective: To determine the applicant understands navigation systems and radar services, can apply that knowledge, manage associated risks, demonstrate appropriate skills, and provide effective instruction.

Note: The evaluator should reference the manufacturer's equipment supplement(s) as necessary for appropriate limitations, procedures, etc.

Knowledge: The applicant demonstrates instructional knowledge by describing and explaining:

AI.II.H.K1	Ground-based navigation (identification, orientation, course determination, equipment, tests, regulations, interference, appropriate use of navigation data, and signal integrity).
AI.II.H.K2	Satellite-based navigation (e.g., equipment, regulations, authorized use of databases, and Receiver Autonomous Integrity Monitoring (RAIM)).
AI.II.H.K3	Radar assistance to visual flight rules (VFR) aircraft (e.g., operations, equipment, available services, traffic advisories).
AI.II.H.K4	Transponder (Mode(s) A, C, and S) and Automatic Dependent Surveillance-Broadcast (ADS-B).

Risk Management: The applicant explains and teaches how to identify and manage risk associated with:

AI.II.H.R1	Management of automated navigation and autoflight systems.
AI.II.H.R2	Distractions, task prioritization, loss of situational awareness, or disorientation.
AI.II.H.R3	Limitations of the navigation system in use.
AI.II.H.R4	Loss of a navigation signal.
AI.II.H.R5	Use of an electronic flight bag (EFB), if used.

Skills: The applicant demonstrates and simultaneously explains how to:

AI.II.H.S1	Use an airborne electronic navigation system.
AI.II.H.S2	Determine the airplane's position using the navigation system.
AI.II.H.S3	Intercept and track a given course, radial, or bearing.
AI.II.H.S4	Recognize and describe the indication of station or waypoint passage.
AI.II.H.S5	Use proper communication procedures when utilizing radar services.

Task I. Navigation and Cross-Country Flight Planning

References: *14 CFR part 91; AIM; Chart Supplements; FAA-H-8083-2, FAA-H-8083-3, FAA-H-8083-9, FAA-H-8083-25, NOTAMs; VFR Navigation Charts*

Objective: To determine the applicant understands navigation and cross-country flight planning, can apply that knowledge, manage associated risks, demonstrate appropriate skills, and provide effective instruction.

Note: *Preparation, presentation, and explanation of a computer-generated flight plan is an acceptable option.*

Knowledge:	The applicant demonstrates instructional knowledge by describing and explaining:
AI.II.I.K1	Route planning, including consideration of different classes and special use airspace (SUA) and selection of appropriate and available navigation/communication systems and facilities.
AI.II.I.K2	Altitude selection accounting for terrain and obstacles, glide distance of airplane, visual flight rules (VFR) cruising altitudes, and effect of wind.
AI.II.I.K3	Plotting a course.
AI.II.I.K4	Power setting selection.
AI.II.I.K5	Calculating:
AI.II.I.K5a	a. Time, climb and descent rates, course, distance, heading, true airspeed, and groundspeed
AI.II.I.K5b	b. Estimated time of arrival, including conversion to universal coordinated time (UTC)
AI.II.I.K5c	c. Fuel requirements, including reserve
AI.II.I.K6	Elements of a VFR flight plan.
AI.II.I.K7	Correlate weather information to make a go/no-go decision.
AI.II.I.K8	Procedures for activating and closing a VFR flight plan.
AI.II.I.K9	Magnetic compass errors.
AI.II.I.K10	Pilotage and dead reckoning.
AI.II.I.K11	Planned calculations versus actual results and required corrections.
AI.II.I.K12	Diversion and lost procedures.
AI.II.I.K13	Inflight intercept procedures.
AI.II.I.K14	Use of an electronic flight bag (EFB), if used.
AI.II.I.K15	Chart symbols.

Risk Management:	The applicant explains and teaches how to identify and manage risk associated with:
AI.II.I.R1	Pilot.
AI.II.I.R2	Aircraft.
AI.II.I.R3	Environment (e.g., weather, airports, airspace, terrain, obstacles).
AI.II.I.R4	External pressures.
AI.II.I.R5	Limitations of air traffic control (ATC) services.
AI.II.I.R6	Fuel planning.

Skills:	The applicant demonstrates and simultaneously explains how to:

Al.II.I.S1	Prepare, present, and explain a cross-country flight plan assigned by the evaluator, including a risk analysis to the first fuel stop.
Al.II.I.S2	Apply pertinent information from appropriate and current aeronautical charts, Chart Supplements; Notices to Air Missions (NOTAMs) relative to airport, runway and taxiway closures; and other flight publications.
Al.II.I.S3	Create a navigation plan and simulate filing a VFR flight plan.
Al.II.I.S4	Recalculate fuel reserves based on a scenario provided by the evaluator.

Task J. 14 CFR and Publications

References: *14 CFR parts 1, 61, 91; 49 CFR part 830; AIM; Chart Supplements; FAA-H-8083-2, FAA-H-8083-3, FAA-H-8083-25; POH/AFM*

Objective: To determine the applicant understands the Code of Federal Regulations and other relevant publications, can apply that knowledge, manage associated risks, demonstrate appropriate skills, and provide effective instruction.

Knowledge:	The applicant demonstrates instructional knowledge by describing and explaining:
Al.II.J.K1	14 CFR parts 1, 61, and 91.
Al.II.J.K2	49 CFR part 830.
Al.II.J.K3	Advisory Circulars, INFOs, and SAFOs.
Al.II.J.K4	Airman Certification Standards or Practical Test Standards.
Al.II.J.K5	Pilot's Operating Handbooks or flight manuals.
Al.II.J.K6	Aeronautical Information Manual (AIM).

Risk Management:	The applicant explains and teaches how to identify and manage risk associated with:
Al.II.J.R1	Use of expired charts, manuals, or publications without current updates.

Skills:	The applicant demonstrates how to:
Al.II.J.S1	Teach at least one of the elements listed in K1 through K6.

Task K. Endorsements and Logbook Entries

References: *14 CFR part 61; AC 61-65; FAA-H-8083-2, FAA-H-8083-3, FAA-H-8083-9, FAA-H-8083-25*

Objective: To determine the applicant understands logbook entries and endorsements, can apply that knowledge, manage associated risks, demonstrate appropriate skills, and provide effective instruction.

Knowledge:	The applicant demonstrates instructional knowledge by describing and explaining:
Al.II.K.K1	Required logbook entries for instruction given.
Al.II.K.K2	Required student pilot pre-solo knowledge test, solo endorsements, and logbook entries.
Al.II.K.K3	Other required pilot logbook endorsements (e.g., Class B Airspace, Special Federal Aviation Regulation (SFAR)).

AI.II.K.K4	Preparation of a recommendation for a pilot practical test, including appropriate logbook entry and relevant certificate/rating application for:
AI.II.K.K4a	a. Initial pilot certification
AI.II.K.K4b	b. Additional pilot certification
AI.II.K.K4c	c. Additional aircraft qualification
AI.II.K.K5	Endorsement of a pilot logbook for the satisfactory completion of an FAA flight review.
AI.II.K.K6	Required flight instructor records.
AI.II.K.K7	Flight instructor renewal and reinstatement requirements.

Risk Management: The applicant is able to identify, assess, and mitigate risk associated with:

AI.II.K.R1	Endorsements without appropriate limitations or expiration dates.

Skills: The applicant demonstrates how to:

AI.II.K.S1	Describe and prepare logbook entries/endorsements required for at least two of the events specified in the elements or sub-elements of K1 through K5.

Task L. Water and Seaplane Characteristics, Seaplane Bases, Maritime Rules, and Aids to Marine Navigation (ASES, AMES)

References: AIM; Chart Supplements; FAA-H-8083-2, FAA-H-8083-9, FAA-H-8083-23, FAA-H-8083-25; POH/AFM; USCG Navigation Rules

Objective: To determine the applicant understands water and seaplane characteristics, seaplane bases, maritime rules, and aids to marine navigation, can apply that knowledge, manage associated risks, demonstrate appropriate skills, and provide effective instruction.

Knowledge: The applicant demonstrates instructional knowledge by describing and explaining:

AI.II.L.K1	Characteristics of a water surface as affected by features, such as:
AI.II.L.K1a	a. Size and location
AI.II.L.K1b	b. Protected and unprotected areas
AI.II.L.K1c	c. Surface wind
AI.II.L.K1d	d. Direction and strength of water current
AI.II.L.K1e	e. Floating and partially submerged debris
AI.II.L.K1f	f. Sandbars, islands, and shoals
AI.II.L.K1g	g. Vessel traffic and wakes
AI.II.L.K1h	h. Direction and height of waves
AI.II.L.K1i	i. Other characteristics specific to the area
AI.II.L.K2	Float and hull construction, and its effect on seaplane performance.
AI.II.L.K3	Causes of porpoising and skipping, and the pilot action needed to prevent or correct these occurrences.
AI.II.L.K4	How to locate and identify seaplane bases on charts or in directories.
AI.II.L.K5	Operating restrictions at various bases.

AI.II.L.K6	Right-of-way, steering, and sailing rules pertinent to seaplane operation.
AI.II.L.K7	Marine navigation aids, such as buoys, beacons, lights, sound signals, and range markers.
AI.II.L.K8	Naval vessel protection zones.
AI.II.L.K9	No wake zones.

Risk Management: The applicant explains and teaches how to identify and manage risk associated with:

AI.II.L.R1	Local conditions.
AI.II.L.R2	Impact of marine traffic.
AI.II.L.R3	Right-of-way and sailing rules pertinent to seaplane operations.
AI.II.L.R4	Limited services and assistance available at seaplane bases.

Skills: The applicant demonstrates and simultaneously explains how to:

AI.II.L.S1	Explain how float and hull construction can affect seaplane performance.
AI.II.L.S2	Describe how to correct for porpoising and skipping.
AI.II.L.S3	Identify marine navigation aids.
AI.II.L.S4	Describe correct right-of-way, steering, and sailing operations.
AI.II.L.S5	Assess the water surface characteristics for the proposed flight.
AI.II.L.S6	Identify restrictions at local seaplane bases.

Task M. Night Operations

References: AIM; FAA-H-8083-2, FAA-H-8083-3, FAA-H-8083-9, FAA-H-8083-25; POH/AFM

Objective: To determine the applicant understands night operations, can apply that knowledge, manage associated risks, demonstrate appropriate skills, and provide effective instruction.

Knowledge: The applicant demonstrates instructional knowledge by describing and explaining:

AI.II.M.K1	Physiological aspects of vision related to night flying.
AI.II.M.K2	Lighting systems identifying airports, runways, taxiways and obstructions, as well as pilot controlled lighting.
AI.II.M.K3	Airplane equipment and lighting requirements for night operations.
AI.II.M.K4	Personal equipment essential for night flight.
AI.II.M.K5	Night orientation, navigation, chart reading techniques and methods for maintaining night vision effectiveness.
AI.II.M.K6	Use of instruments to verify the aircraft attitude at night.
AI.II.M.K7	Visual illusions at night.
AI.II.M.K8	Night taxi operations.
AI.II.M.K9	Interpretation of traffic position and direction based solely on position lights.

Risk Management: The applicant explains and teaches how to identify and manage risk associated with:

AI.II.M.R1   Inoperative equipment.

AI.II.M.R2   Weather considerations specific to night operations.

AI.II.M.R3   Collision hazards.

AI.II.M.R4   Distractions, task prioritization, loss of situational awareness, or disorientation.

AI.II.M.R5   Effect of visual illusions and night adaptation during all phases of night flying.

AI.II.M.R6   Runway incursion.

AI.II.M.R7   Night currency versus proficiency.

Skills: The applicant demonstrates how to:

AI.II.M.S1   Teach at least one of the elements listed in K1 through K9.

Task N. High Altitude Operations - Supplemental Oxygen

References: 14 CFR part 91; AC 61-107; AIM; FAA-H-8083-2, FAA-H-8083-3, FAA-H-8083-9, FAA-H-8083-25; POH/AFM

Objective: To determine the applicant exhibits satisfactory knowledge, risk management, and skills associated with flight at higher altitudes where supplemental oxygen is required or recommended, can apply that knowledge, manage associated risks, demonstrate appropriate skills, and provide effective instruction.

Knowledge: The applicant demonstrates instructional knowledge by describing and explaining:

AI.II.N.K 1   Regulatory requirements for supplemental oxygen use by flight crew and passengers.

AI.II.N.K2   Physiological factors, including:

AI.II.N.K2a   a. Impairment

AI.II.N.K2b   b. Symptoms of hypoxia

AI.II.N.K2c   c. Time of useful consciousness (TUC)

AI.II.N.K3   Operational factors, including:

AI.II.N.K3a   a. Characteristics, limitations, and applicability of continuous flow, demand, and pressure-demand oxygen systems

AI.II.N.K3b   b. Differences between and identification of "aviator's breathing oxygen" and other types of oxygen

AI.II.N.K3c   c. Precautions when using supplemental oxygen systems

Risk Management: The applicant explains and teaches how to identify and manage risk associated with:

AI.II.N.R1   High altitude flight.

AI.II.N.R2   Use of supplemental oxygen.

AI.II.N.R3   Management of compressed gas containers.

AI.II.N.R4   Combustion hazards in an oxygen-rich environment.

Skills:	The applicant demonstrates and simultaneously explains how to:
AI.II.N.S1	Provide an adequate briefing on use of supplemental oxygen equipment.
AI.II.N.S2	Operate or simulate operation of the installed or portable oxygen equipment in the aircraft, if installed or available.
AI.II.N.S3	Determine the quantity of supplemental oxygen required in a scenario given by the evaluator.

Task O. High Altitude Operations - Pressurization

References:	AC 61-107; AIM; FAA-H-8083-2, FAA-H-8083-3, FAA-H-8083-9, FAA-H-8083-25; POH/AFM
Objective:	To determine the applicant understands flight in pressurized aircraft at high altitudes, can apply that knowledge, manage associated risks, demonstrate appropriate skills, and provide effective instruction.

Knowledge:	The applicant demonstrates instructional knowledge by describing and explaining:
AI.II.O.K1	Fundamental concepts of aircraft pressurization system, including failure modes.
AI.II.O.K2	Physiological factors, including:
AI.II.O.K2a	a. Impairment
AI.II.O.K2b	b. Symptoms of hypoxia
AI.II.O.K2c	c. Time of useful consciousness (TUC)
AI.II.O.K2d	d. Effects of rapid decompression on crew and passengers

Risk Management:	The applicant explains and teaches how to identify and manage risk associated with:
AI.II.O.R1	High altitude flight.
AI.II.O.R2	Malfunction of pressurization system, if equipment is installed.

Skills:	The applicant demonstrates and simultaneously explains how to:
AI.II.O.S1	Operate the pressurization system, if equipment is installed.
AI.II.O.S2	Respond appropriately to simulated pressurization malfunctions, if equipment is installed.

Task P. One Engine Inoperative (OEI) Performance (AMEL, AMES)

References:	FAA-H-8083-2, FAA-H-8083-3, FAA-H-8083-9, FAA-H-8083-25; FAA-P-8740-66; POH/AFM
Objective:	To determine the applicant understands elements related to multiengine performance, can apply that knowledge, manage associated risks, demonstrate appropriate skills, and provide effective instruction.
Note:	Evaluator assesses the applicant's knowledge of at least two knowledge elements from this Task.

Knowledge:	The applicant demonstrates instructional knowledge by describing and explaining:
AI.II.P.K1	Proficient use of appropriate performance charts, tables, graphs, or other data to determine airplane performance and limitations for all phases of flight.
AI.II.P.K2	Effects of exceeding limitations.
AI.II.P.K3	Effects of atmospheric conditions on performance.

AI.II.P.K4	Factors to be considered to determine required performance is within the airplane's single and multiengine cababilities.
AI.II.P.K5	Aerodynamics of OEI operation including:
AI.II.P.K5a	a. Critical engine
AI.II.P.K5b	b. Effects of bank angle on V_{MC}
AI.II.P.K5c	c. Zero side slip
AI.II.P.K5d	d. Reasons for loss of directional control
AI.II.P.K6	The relationship between minimum control speed (V_{MC}) and stall speed and the effect of density altitude on that relationship.
AI.II.P.K7	How to determine the best course of action after an engine failure.

Risk Management: The applicant explains and teaches how to identify and manage risk associated with:

AI.II.P.R1	Exceeding the critical angle of attack.
AI.II.P.R2	Loss of directional control.
AI.II.P.R3	Flying over terrain that exceeds the single engine service ceiling.
AI.II.P.R4	Fuel management.

Skills: The applicant demonstrates and simultaneously explains how to:

| AI.II.P.S1 | Compute the expected single engine climb performance. |

Area of Operation III. Preflight Preparation

Note: *The evaluator must select at least one Task from this Area of Operation.*

Task A. Pilot Qualifications

References: *14 CFR parts 61, 68, 91; AC 60-28, AC 68-1; FAA-H-8083-2, FAA-H-8083-3, FAA-H-8083-23, FAA-H-8083-25; POH/AFM*

Objective: To determine the applicant understands pilot training and qualification requirements for different levels of pilot certificate including student pilot, sport pilot, recreational pilot, private pilot, commercial pilot, and flight instructor; can apply that knowledge, manage associated risks, demonstrate appropriate skills, and provide effective instruction.

Knowledge:	The applicant demonstrates instructional knowledge by describing and explaining:
AI.III.A.K1	Certification, currency, and recordkeeping requirements, including training and logbook entries.
AI.III.A.K2	Privileges and limitations of pilot certificates and ratings at student pilot, sport, recreational, private, commercial, and flight instructor levels.
AI.III.A.K3	Medical certificates: class, expiration, privileges, temporary disqualifications, and operations under BasicMed.
AI.III.A.K4	Documents pilots must possess to exercise privileges of the specified certificate(s) and rating(s).

Risk Management:	The applicant explains and teaches how to identify and manage risk associated with:
AI.III.A.R1	Proficiency versus currency.
AI.III.A.R2	Flying unfamiliar aircraft or operating with unfamiliar flight display systems and avionics.

Skills:	The applicant demonstrates how to:
AI.III.A.S1	Deliver instruction on at least two of the elements specified in K1 through K4.

Task B. Airworthiness Requirements

References: *14 CFR parts 23, 39, 43, 91; FAA-H-8083-2, FAA-H-8083-3, FAA-H-8083-9, FAA-H-8083-23, FAA-H-8083-25*

Objective: To determine the applicant understands airworthiness requirements, including aircraft certificates, can apply that knowledge, manage associated risks, demonstrate appropriate skills, and provide effective instruction.

Knowledge:	The applicant demonstrates instructional knowledge by describing and explaining:
AI.III.B.K1	General airworthiness requirements and compliance for airplanes, including:
AI.III.B.K1a	a. Location and expiration dates of required aircraft certificates
AI.III.B.K1b	b. Required inspections and aircraft logbook documentation
AI.III.B.K1c	c. Airworthiness Directives and Special Airworthiness Information Bulletins
AI.III.B.K1d	d. Purpose and procedure for obtaining a special flight permit
AI.III.B.K2	Pilot-performed preventive maintenance.
AI.III.B.K3	Equipment requirements for day and night VFR flight, including:

AI.III.B.K3a	a. Flying with inoperative equipment
AI.III.B.K3b	b. Using an approved Minimum Equipment List (MEL)
AI.III.B.K3c	c. Kinds of Operation Equipment List (KOEL)
AI.III.B.K3d	d. Required discrepancy records or placards
AI.III.B.K4	Standard and special airworthiness certificates and their associated operational limitations.

Risk Management: The applicant explains and teaches how to identify and manage risk associated with:

AI.III.B.R1	Inoperative equipment discovered prior to flight.

Skills: The applicant demonstrates and simultaneously explains how to:

AI.III.B.S1	Locate and describe airplane airworthiness and registration information.
AI.III.B.S2	Determine the airplane is airworthy in the scenario given by the evaluator.
AI.III.B.S3	Apply appropriate procedures for operating with inoperative equipment in a scenario given by the evaluator.

Task C. Weather Information

References: 14 CFR part 91; AC 91-92; AIM; FAA-H-8083-2, FAA-H-8083-3, FAA-H-8083-9, FAA-H-8083-25, FAA-H-8083-28

Objective: To determine the applicant understands weather information, can apply that knowledge, manage associated risks, demonstrate appropriate skills, and provide effective instruction.

Note: If K2 is selected, the evaluator must assess the applicant's knowledge of at least three sub-elements.

Note: If K3 is selected, the evaluator must assess the applicant's knowledge of at least three sub-elements.

Knowledge: The applicant demonstrates instructional knowledge by describing and explaining:

AI.III.C.K1	Sources of weather data (e.g., National Weather Service, Flight Service) for flight planning purposes.
AI.III.C.K2	Acceptable weather products and resources required for preflight planning, current and forecast weather for departure, en route, and arrival phases of flight such as:
AI.III.C.K2a	a. Airport Observations (METAR and SPECI) and Pilot Observations (PIREP)
AI.III.C.K2b	b. Surface Analysis Chart, Ceiling and Visibility Chart (CVA)
AI.III.C.K2c	c. Terminal Aerodrome Forecasts (TAF)
AI.III.C.K2d	d. Graphical Forecasts for Aviation (GFA)
AI.III.C.K2e	e. Wind and Temperature Aloft Forecast (FB)
AI.III.C.K2f	f. Convective Outlook (AC)
AI.III.C.K2g	g. Inflight Aviation Weather Advisories including Airmen's Meteorological Information (AIRMET), Significant Meteorological Information (SIGMET), and Convective SIGMET
AI.III.C.K3	Meteorology applicable to the departure, en route, alternate, and destination under visual flight rules (VFR) in Visual Meteorological Conditions (VMC), including expected climate and hazardous conditions such as:
AI.III.C.K3a	a. Atmospheric composition and stability

AI.III.C.K3b	b. Wind (e.g., windshear, mountain wave, factors affecting wind, etc.)
AI.III.C.K3c	c. Temperature and heat exchange
AI.III.C.K3d	d. Moisture/precipitation
AI.III.C.K3e	e. Weather system formation, including air masses and fronts
AI.III.C.K3f	f. Clouds
AI.III.C.K3g	g. Turbulence
AI.III.C.K3h	h. Thunderstorms and microbursts
AI.III.C.K3i	i. Icing and freezing level information
AI.III.C.K3j	j. Fog/mist
AI.III.C.K3k	k. Frost
AI.III.C.K3l	l. Obstructions to visibility (e.g., smoke, haze, volcanic ash, etc.)
AI.III.C.K4	Flight deck instrument displays of digital weather and aeronautical information.

Risk Management: The applicant explains and teaches how to identify and manage risk associated with:

AI.III.C.R1	Making the go/no-go and continue/divert decisions, including:
AI.III.C.R1a	a. Circumstances that would make diversion prudent
AI.III.C.R1b	b. Personal weather minimums
AI.III.C.R1c	c. Hazardous weather conditions, including known or forecast icing or turbulence aloft
AI.III.C.R2	Use and limitations of:
AI.III.C.R2a	a. Installed onboard weather equipment
AI.III.C.R2b	b. Aviation weather reports and forecasts
AI.III.C.R2c	c. Inflight weather resources

Skills: The applicant demonstrates and simultaneously explains how to:

AI.III.C.S1	Use available aviation weather resources to obtain an adequate weather briefing.
AI.III.C.S2	Analyze the implications of at least three of the conditions listed in K3a through K3l, using actual weather or weather conditions provided by the evaluator.
AI.III.C.S3	Correlate weather information to make a go/no-go decision.

Area of Operation IV. Preflight Lesson on a Maneuver to be Performed in Flight

Note: *The evaluator asks the applicant to present a preflight lesson on the selected maneuver as the lesson would be taught to a student and determines the outcome of this Task before the flight portion of the practical test. Previously developed lesson plans from the instructor applicant's library may be used.*

Task A. Maneuver Lesson

References: *FAA-H-8083-2, FAA-H-8083-3, FAA-H-8083-9, FAA-H-8083-23, FAA-H-8083-25; POH/AFM*

Objective: To determine the applicant understands the elements associated with a maneuver Task selected from Area of Operation VII through Area of Operation XII (ASEL, ASES) or Area of Operation VII through Area of Operation XIII (AMEL, AMES) and applies that knowledge when delivering ground instruction.

Knowledge:	The applicant demonstrates instructional knowledge by describing and explaining:
AI.IV.A.K1	Purpose of the maneuver.
AI.IV.A.K2	Elements of the maneuver and the associated common errors.
AI.IV.A.K3	Desired outcome(s), including completion standards.

Risk Management:	The applicant explains and teaches how to identify and manage risk associated with:
AI.IV.A.R1	The selected maneuver Task.

Skills:	The applicant exhibits the skill to:
AI.IV.A.S1	Deliver instruction on the selected maneuver using a lesson plan, teaching methods, and teaching aids, as appropriate, that incorporate K1 through K3.

Area of Operation V. Preflight Procedures

Note: *The evaluator must select at least one Task from this Area of Operation.*

Task A. Preflight Assessment

References: *FAA-H-8083-2, FAA-H-8083-3, FAA-H-8083-9, FAA-H-8083-23, FAA-H-8083-25, FAA-H-8083-28; POH/AFM*

Objective: To determine the applicant understands preflight assessment, can apply that knowledge, manage associated risks, demonstrate appropriate skills, and provide effective instruction.

Knowledge:	The applicant demonstrates instructional knowledge by describing and explaining:
AI.V.A.K1	Pilot self-assessment.
AI.V.A.K2	Determining that the airplane to be used is appropriate and airworthy.
AI.V.A.K3	Airplane preflight inspection, including:
AI.V.A.K3a	a. Which items should be inspected
AI.V.A.K3b	b. The reasons for checking each item
AI.V.A.K3c	c. How to detect possible defects
AI.V.A.K3d	d. The associated regulations
AI.V.A.K4	Environmental factors, including weather, terrain, route selection, and obstructions.

Risk Management:	The applicant explains and teaches how to identify and manage risk associated with:
AI.V.A.R1	Pilot.
AI.V.A.R2	Aircraft.
AI.V.A.R3	Environment (e.g., weather, airports, airspace, terrain, obstacles).
AI.V.A.R4	External pressures.
AI.V.A.R5	Aviation security concerns.

Skills:	The applicant demonstrates and simultaneously explains how to:
AI.V.A.S1	Inspect the airplane with reference to an appropriate checklist.
AI.V.A.S2	Verify the airplane is in condition for safe flight and conforms to its type design.
AI.V.A.S3	Perform self-assessment.
AI.V.A.S4	Continue to assess the environment for safe flight.

Task B. Flight Deck Management

References: *14 CFR part 91; AC 120-71; FAA-H-8083-2, FAA-H-8083-3, FAA-H-8083-9, FAA-H-8083-23, FAA-H-8083-25; POH/AFM*

Objective: To determine the applicant understands flight deck management, can apply that knowledge, manage associated risks, demonstrate appropriate skills, and provide effective instruction.

Note: *See Appendix 2: Safety of Flight.*

Knowledge:	The applicant demonstrates instructional knowledge by describing and explaining:
AI.V.B.K1	Passenger briefing requirements, including operation and required use of safety restraint systems.
AI.V.B.K2	Use of appropriate checklists.
AI.V.B.K3	Requirements for current and appropriate navigation data.
AI.V.B.K4	Securing items and cargo.

Risk Management:	The applicant explains and teaches how to identify and manage risk associated with:
AI.V.B.R1	Use of systems or equipment, including automation and portable electronic devices.
AI.V.B.R2	Inoperative equipment.
AI.V.B.R3	Passenger distractions.

Skills:	The applicant demonstrates and simultaneously explains how to:
AI.V.B.S1	Secure all items in the aircraft.
AI.V.B.S2	Conduct an appropriate passenger briefing, including identifying the pilot-in-command (PIC), use of safety belts, shoulder harnesses, doors, passenger conduct, sterile aircraft, propeller blade avoidance, and emergency procedures.
AI.V.B.S3	Properly program and manage the aircraft's automation, as applicable.
AI.V.B.S4	Appropriately manage risks by utilizing ADM, including SRM/CRM.

Task C. Engine Starting

References: FAA-H-8083-2, FAA-H-8083-3, FAA-H-8083-9, FAA-H-8083-23, FAA-H-8083-25; POH/AFM

Objective: To determine the applicant understands engine starting, can apply that knowledge, manage associated risks, demonstrate appropriate skills, and provide effective instruction.

Knowledge:	The applicant demonstrates instructional knowledge by describing and explaining:
AI.V.C.K1	Starting under various conditions.
AI.V.C.K2	Starting the engine(s) by use of external power.
AI.V.C.K3	Engine limitations as they relate to starting.

Risk Management:	The applicant explains and teaches how to identify and manage risk associated with:
AI.V.C.R1	Propeller safety.
AI.V.C.R2	Use of external power unit.
AI.V.C.R3	Limitations during starting.

Skills:	The applicant demonstrates and simultaneously explains how to:
AI.V.C.S1	Position the airplane properly considering structures, other aircraft, wind, and the safety of nearby persons and property.
AI.V.C.S2	Complete the appropriate checklist(s).

Task D. Taxiing, Airport Signs, and Lighting (ASEL, AMEL)

References: AC 91-73; AIM; Chart Supplements; FAA-H-8083-2, FAA-H-8083-3, FAA-H-8083-9, FAA-H-8083-25; POH/AFM

Objective: To determine the applicant understands taxiing an airplane, can apply that knowledge, manage associated risks, demonstrate appropriate skills, and provide effective instruction.

Knowledge:	The applicant demonstrates instructional knowledge by describing and explaining:
AI.V.D.K1	Elements of safe taxi operations.
AI.V.D.K2	Current airport aeronautical references and information resources such as the Chart Supplement, airport diagram, and Notices to Air Missions (NOTAMs).
AI.V.D.K3	Taxi instructions/clearances.
AI.V.D.K4	Airport markings, signs, and lights.
AI.V.D.K5	Visual indicators for wind.
AI.V.D.K6	Aircraft lighting, as appropriate.
AI.V.D.K7	Procedures for:
AI.V.D.K7a	a. Appropriate flight deck activities prior to taxi, including route planning and identifying the location of Hot Spots
AI.V.D.K7b	b. Radio communications at towered and nontowered airports
AI.V.D.K7c	c. Entering or crossing runways
AI.V.D.K7d	d. Night taxi operations
AI.V.D.K7e	e. Low visibility taxi operations

Risk Management:	The applicant explains and teaches how to identify and manage risk associated with:
AI.V.D.R1	Activities and distractions.
AI.V.D.R2	Confirmation or expectation bias as related to taxi instructions.
AI.V.D.R3	A taxi route or departure runway change.
AI.V.D.R4	Runway incursion.

Skills:	The applicant demonstrates and simultaneously explains how to:
AI.V.D.S1	Receive and correctly read back clearances/instructions, if applicable.
AI.V.D.S2	Use an airport diagram or taxi chart during taxi, if published, and maintain situational awareness.
AI.V.D.S3	Position the flight controls for the existing wind, if applicable.
AI.V.D.S4	Complete the appropriate checklist(s).
AI.V.D.S5	Perform a brake check immediately after the airplane begins moving.
AI.V.D.S6	Maintain positive control of the airplane during ground operations by controlling direction and speed without excessive use of brakes.
AI.V.D.S7	Comply with airport/taxiway markings, signals, and air traffic control (ATC) clearances and instructions.
AI.V.D.S8	Position the airplane properly relative to hold lines.

Task E. Taxiing and Sailing (ASES, AMES)

References: AC 91-73; AIM; Chart Supplements; FAA-H-8083-2, FAA-H-8083-9, FAA-H-8083-23, FAA-H-8083-25; POH/AFM; USCG Navigation Rules

Objective: To determine the applicant understands taxiing and sailing, can apply that knowledge, manage associated risks, demonstrate appropriate skills, and provide effective instruction.

Knowledge:	The applicant demonstrates instructional knowledge by describing and explaining:
AI.V.E.K1	Procedures for various types of taxiing and sailing.
AI.V.E.K2	Current airport aeronautical references and information resources such as the Chart Supplement, airport diagram, and Notices to Air Missions (NOTAMs).
AI.V.E.K3	Taxi instructions/clearances.
AI.V.E.K4	Airport/seaplane base markings, signs, and lights.
AI.V.E.K5	Visual indicators for wind.
AI.V.E.K6	Airplane lighting.
AI.V.E.K7	Procedures for:
AI.V.E.K7a	a. Appropriate flight deck activities during taxiing or sailing
AI.V.E.K7b	b. Radio communications at towered and nontowered seaplane bases

Risk Management:	The applicant explains and teaches how to identify and manage risk associated with:
AI.V.E.R1	Activities and distractions.
AI.V.E.R2	Porpoising and skipping.
AI.V.E.R3	Low visibility taxi and sailing operations.
AI.V.E.R4	Other aircraft, vessels, and hazards.
AI.V.E.R5	Confirmation or expectation bias as related to taxi instructions.

Skills:	The applicant demonstrates and simultaneously explains how to:
AI.V.E.S1	Receive and correctly read back clearances/instructions, if applicable.
AI.V.E.S2	Use an appropriate airport diagram or taxi chart, if published.
AI.V.E.S3	Comply with seaplane base/airport/taxiway markings, signals, and signs.
AI.V.E.S4	Depart the dock/mooring buoy or beach/ramp in a safe manner, considering wind, current, traffic, and hazards.
AI.V.E.S5	Complete the appropriate checklist(s).
AI.V.E.S6	Position the flight controls, flaps, doors, water rudders, and power correctly for the existing conditions to follow the desired course while sailing and to prevent or correct for porpoising and skipping during step taxi.
AI.V.E.S7	Exhibit procedures for steering and maneuvering while maintaining proper situational awareness and desired orientation, path, and position while taxiing using idle, plow, or step taxi technique, as appropriate.
AI.V.E.S8	Plan and follow the most favorable taxi or sailing course for current conditions.
AI.V.E.S9	Abide by right-of-way rules, maintain positive airplane control, proper speed, and separation between other aircraft, vessels, and persons.

AI.V.E.S10	Comply with applicable taxi elements in Task D if the practical test is conducted in an amphibious airplane.

Task F. Before Takeoff Check

References: *FAA-H-8083-2, FAA-H-8083-3, FAA-H-8083-9, FAA-H-8083-23, FAA-H-8083-25; POH/AFM*

Objective: To determine the applicant understands before takeoff checks, can apply that knowledge, manage associated risks, demonstrate appropriate skills, and provide effective instruction.

Knowledge:	The applicant demonstrates instructional knowledge by describing and explaining:
AI.V.F.K1	Purpose of before takeoff checklist items, including:
AI.V.F.K1a	a. Reasons for checking each item
AI.V.F.K1b	b. Detecting malfunctions
AI.V.F.K1c	c. Ensuring the aircraft is in safe operating condition as recommended by the manufacturer

Risk Management:	The applicant explains and teaches how to identify and manage risk associated with:
AI.V.F.R1	Division of attention while conducting before takeoff checks.
AI.V.F.R2	Unexpected runway changes by air traffic control (ATC).
AI.V.F.R3	Wake turbulence.
AI.V.F.R4	Potential powerplant failure during takeoff or other malfunction considering operational factors such as airplane characteristics, runway/takeoff path length, surface conditions, environmental conditions, and obstructions.

Skills:	The applicant demonstrates and simultaneously explains how to:
AI.V.F.S1	Review takeoff performance.
AI.V.F.S2	Complete the appropriate checklist(s).
AI.V.F.S3	Position the airplane appropriately considering wind direction and the presence of any aircraft, vessels, or buildings as applicable.
AI.V.F.S4	Divide attention inside and outside the flight deck.
AI.V.F.S5	Verify that engine parameters and airplane configuration are suitable.

Area of Operation VI. Airport and Seaplane Base Operations

Note: The evaluator must select at least one Task from this Area of Operation.

Task A. Communications, Light Signals, and Runway Lighting Systems

References: *14 CFR part 91; AIM; FAA-H-8083-2, FAA-H-8083-3, FAA-H-8083-9, FAA-H-8083-25*

Objective: To determine the applicant understands communications, ATC light signals, and runway lighting systems and can apply that knowledge, manage associated risks, demonstrate appropriate skills, and provide effective instruction.

Knowledge:	The applicant demonstrates instructional knowledge by describing and explaining:
AI.VI.A.K1	How to obtain appropriate radio frequencies.
AI.VI.A.K2	Proper radio communication procedures and air traffic control (ATC) phraseology.
AI.VI.A.K3	ATC light signal recognition.
AI.VI.A.K4	Appropriate use of transponder(s).
AI.VI.A.K5	Lost communication procedures.
AI.VI.A.K6	Equipment issues that could cause loss of communication.
AI.VI.A.K7	Radar assistance.
AI.VI.A.K8	Runway Status Lighting Systems.
AI.VI.A.K9	Common errors related to this Task.

Risk Management:	The applicant explains and teaches how to identify and manage risk associated with:
AI.VI.A.R1	Communication.
AI.VI.A.R2	Deciding if and when to declare an emergency.

Skills:	The applicant demonstrates and simultaneously explains how to:
AI.VI.A.S1	Select and activate appropriate frequencies.
AI.VI.A.S2	Transmit using standard phraseology and procedures as specified in the Aeronautical Information Manual (AIM) and Pilot/Controller Glossary.
AI.VI.A.S3	Acknowledge radio communications and comply with ATC instructions or as directed by the evaluator.
AI.VI.A.S4	Analyze and correct common errors related to this Task.

Task B. Traffic Patterns

References: *14 CFR part 91; AIM; FAA-H-8083-2, FAA-H-8083-3, FAA-H-8083-9, FAA-H-8083-25*

Objective: To determine the applicant understands traffic patterns, can apply that knowledge, manage associated risks, demonstrate appropriate skills, and provide effective instruction.

Knowledge:	The applicant demonstrates instructional knowledge by describing and explaining:
AI.VI.B.K1	Towered and nontowered airport operations.
AI.VI.B.K2	Traffic pattern selection for the current conditions.

AI.VI.B.K3	Right-of-way rules.
AI.VI.B.K4	Use of automated weather and airport information.
AI.VI.B.K5	Common errors related to this Task.

Risk Management: The applicant explains and teaches how to identify and manage risk associated with:

AI.VI.B.R1	Collision hazards.
AI.VI.B.R2	Distractions, task prioritization, loss of situational awareness, or disorientation.
AI.VI.B.R3	Windshear and wake turbulence.

Skills: The applicant demonstrates and simultaneously explains how to:

AI.VI.B.S1	Identify and interpret airport/seaplane base runways, taxiways, markings, signs, and lighting.
AI.VI.B.S2	Comply with recommended traffic pattern procedures.
AI.VI.B.S3	Correct for wind drift to maintain the proper ground track.
AI.VI.B.S4	Maintain orientation with the runway/landing area in use.
AI.VI.B.S5	Maintain traffic pattern altitude, ±100 feet, and the appropriate airspeed, ±10 knots.
AI.VI.B.S6	Maintain situational awareness and proper spacing from other aircraft in the traffic pattern.
AI.VI.B.S7	Analyze and correct common errors related to this Task.

Area of Operation VII. Takeoffs, Landings, and Go-Arounds

Note: *The evaluator must select at least two takeoff and two landing Tasks from Area of Operation VII, Takeoffs, Landings, and Go-Arounds.*

Task A. Normal Takeoff and Climb

References: *AIM; FAA-H-8083-2, FAA-H-8083-3, FAA-H-8083-9, FAA-H-8083-23, FAA-H-8083-25; POH/AFM*

Objective: To determine the applicant understands normal takeoff and climb, can apply that knowledge, manage associated risks, demonstrate appropriate skills, and provide effective instruction.

Note: *If a crosswind condition does not exist, the applicant's knowledge of crosswind elements must be evaluated through oral testing.*

Knowledge:	The applicant demonstrates instructional knowledge by describing and explaining:
AI.VII.A.K1	Procedures for normal and crosswind takeoff.
AI.VII.A.K2	Effects of atmospheric conditions, including wind, on takeoff and climb performance.
AI.VII.A.K3	Best angle of climb speed (V_X) and best rate of climb speed (V_Y).
AI.VII.A.K4	Appropriate airplane configuration.
AI.VII.A.K5	Common errors related to this Task.

Risk Management:	The applicant explains and teaches how to identify and manage risk associated with:
AI.VII.A.R1	Selection of runway based on pilot capability, airplane performance and limitations, available distance, and wind.
AI.VII.A.R2	Effects of:
AI.VII.A.R2a	a. Crosswind
AI.VII.A.R2b	b. Windshear
AI.VII.A.R2c	c. Tailwind
AI.VII.A.R2d	d. Wake turbulence
AI.VII.A.R2e	e. Takeoff surface/condition
AI.VII.A.R3	Abnormal operations, including planning for:
AI.VII.A.R3a	a. Rejected takeoff
AI.VII.A.R3b	b. Potential engine failure in takeoff/climb phase of flight
AI.VII.A.R4	Collision hazards.
AI.VII.A.R5	Low altitude maneuvering, including stall, spin, or controlled flight into terrain (CFIT).
AI.VII.A.R6	Distractions, task prioritization, loss of situational awareness, or disorientation.
AI.VII.A.R7	Runway incursion.

Skills:	The applicant demonstrates and simultaneously explains how to:
AI.VII.A.S1	Complete the appropriate checklist(s).
AI.VII.A.S2	Make radio calls as appropriate.
AI.VII.A.S3	Verify assigned/correct runway or takeoff path.

AI.VII.A.S4	Determine wind direction with or without visible wind direction indicators.
AI.VII.A.S5	Position the flight controls for the existing wind, if applicable.
AI.VII.A.S6	Clear the area, taxi into takeoff position, and align the airplane on the runway centerline (ASEL, AMEL) or takeoff path (ASES, AMES).
AI.VII.A.S7	Retract the water rudders, as appropriate (ASES, AMES).
AI.VII.A.S8	Advance the throttle smoothly to takeoff power and confirm proper engine and flight instrument indications prior to rotation.
AI.VII.A.S9	Avoid excessive water spray on the propeller(s) (ASES, AMES).
AI.VII.A.S10	Establish and maintain the most efficient planing/lift-off attitude, and correct for porpoising or skipping (ASES, AMES).
AI.VII.A.S11	Rotate and lift off at the recommended airspeed and accelerate to V_Y.
AI.VII.A.S12	Establish a pitch attitude to maintain the manufacturer's recommended speed or V_Y, ±5 knots.
AI.VII.A.S13	Configure the airplane in accordance with manufacturer's guidance.
AI.VII.A.S14	Maintain V_Y ±5 knots to a safe maneuvering altitude.
AI.VII.A.S15	Maintain directional control and proper wind-drift correction throughout takeoff and climb.
AI.VII.A.S16	Comply with noise abatement procedures, as applicable.
AI.VII.A.S17	Analyze and correct common errors related to this Task.

Task B. Normal Approach and Landing

References: AIM; FAA-H-8083-2, FAA-H-8083-3, FAA-H-8083-9, FAA-H-8083-23, FAA-H-8083-25; POH/AFM

Objective: To determine the applicant understands normal approach and landing, can apply that knowledge, manage associated risks, demonstrate appropriate skills, and provide effective instruction.

Note: If a crosswind condition does not exist, the applicant's knowledge of crosswind elements must be evaluated through oral testing.

Knowledge:	The applicant demonstrates instructional knowledge by describing and explaining:
AI.VII.B.K1	Procedures for normal and crosswind approach and landing.
AI.VII.B.K2	A stabilized approach, including energy management concepts.
AI.VII.B.K3	Effects of atmospheric conditions, including wind, on approach and landing performance.
AI.VII.B.K4	Wind correction techniques on approach and landing.
AI.VII.B.K5	Common errors related to this Task.

Risk Management:	The applicant explains and teaches how to identify and manage risk associated with:
AI.VII.B.R1	Selection of runway/landing surface, approach path, and touchdown area based on pilot capability, aircraft performance and limitations, available distance, and wind.
AI.VII.B.R2	Effects of:
AI.VII.B.R2a	a. Crosswind
AI.VII.B.R2b	b. Windshear
AI.VII.B.R2c	c. Tailwind

AI.VII.B.R2d	d. Wake turbulence
AI.VII.B.R2e	e. Landing surface/condition
AI.VII.B.R3	Planning for:
AI.VII.B.R3a	a. Rejected landing and go-around
AI.VII.B.R3b	b. Land and hold short operations (LAHSO)
AI.VII.B.R4	Collision hazards.
AI.VII.B.R5	Low altitude maneuvering, including stall, spin, or controlled flight into terrain (CFIT).
AI.VII.B.R6	Distractions, task prioritization, loss of situational awareness, or disorientation.

Skills:	The applicant demonstrates and simultaneously explains how to:
AI.VII.B.S1	Complete the appropriate checklist(s).
AI.VII.B.S2	Make radio calls as appropriate.
AI.VII.B.S3	Ensure the airplane is aligned with the correct/assigned runway or landing surface.
AI.VII.B.S4	Scan the runway or landing surface and adjoining area for traffic and obstructions.
AI.VII.B.S5	Select and aim for a suitable touchdown point considering the wind conditions, landing surface, and obstructions.
AI.VII.B.S6	Establish the recommended approach and landing configuration, airspeed, and trim, and adjust pitch attitude and power as required to maintain a stabilized approach.
AI.VII.B.S7	Maintain manufacturer's published approach airspeed or in its absence not more than 1.3 times the stalling speed or the minimum steady flight speed in the landing configuration (V_{SO}), ±5 knots with gust factor applied.
AI.VII.B.S8	Maintain directional control and appropriate crosswind correction throughout the approach and landing.
AI.VII.B.S9	Make smooth, timely, and correct control application during round out and touchdown.
AI.VII.B.S10	Touch down at a proper pitch attitude, within 200 feet beyond or on the specified point, with no side drift, and with the airplane's longitudinal axis aligned with and over the runway center/landing path.
AI.VII.B.S11	Execute a timely go-around if the approach cannot be made within the tolerances specified above or for any other condition that may result in an unsafe approach or landing.
AI.VII.B.S12	Analyze and correct common errors related to this Task.

Task C. Soft-Field Takeoff and Climb (ASEL)

References: AIM; FAA-H-8083-2, FAA-H-8083-3, FAA-H-8083-9, FAA-H-8083-25; POH/AFM

Objective: To determine the applicant understands soft-field takeoff and climb, can apply that knowledge, manage associated risks, demonstrate appropriate skills, and provide effective instruction.

Knowledge:	The applicant demonstrates instructional knowledge by describing and explaining:
AI.VII.C.K1	Purpose of and procedures for soft-field takeoff and climb.
AI.VII.C.K2	Effects of atmospheric conditions, including wind, on takeoff and climb performance.
AI.VII.C.K3	Best angle of climb speed (V_X) and best rate of climb speed (V_Y).
AI.VII.C.K4	Appropriate airplane configuration.

AI.VII.C.K5	Ground effect.
AI.VII.C.K6	Importance of weight transfer from wheels to wings.
AI.VII.C.K7	Left turning tendencies.
AI.VII.C.K8	Common errors related to this Task.

Risk Management: The applicant explains and teaches how to identify and manage risk associated with:

AI.VII.C.R1	Selection of runway based on pilot capability, airplane performance and limitations, available distance, and wind.
AI.VII.C.R2	Effects of:
AI.VII.C.R2a	a. Crosswind
AI.VII.C.R2b	b. Windshear
AI.VII.C.R2c	c. Tailwind
AI.VII.C.R2d	d. Wake turbulence
AI.VII.C.R2e	e. Runway surface/condition
AI.VII.C.R3	Abnormal operations, including planning for:
AI.VII.C.R3a	a. Rejected takeoff
AI.VII.C.R3b	b. Potential engine failure in takeoff/climb phase of flight
AI.VII.C.R4	Collision hazards.
AI.VII.C.R5	Low altitude maneuvering, including stall, spin, or controlled flight into terrain (CFIT).
AI.VII.C.R6	Distractions, task prioritization, loss of situational awareness, or disorientation.

Skills: The applicant demonstrates and simultaneously explains how to:

AI.VII.C.S1	Complete the appropriate checklist(s).
AI.VII.C.S2	Make radio calls as appropriate.
AI.VII.C.S3	Verify assigned/correct runway.
AI.VII.C.S4	Determine wind direction with or without visible wind direction indicators.
AI.VII.C.S5	Position the flight controls for the existing wind, if applicable.
AI.VII.C.S6	Clear the area, maintain necessary flight control inputs, taxi into takeoff position and align the airplane on the runway centerline without stopping, while advancing the throttle smoothly to takeoff power.
AI.VII.C.S7	Confirm takeoff power and proper engine and flight instrument indications.
AI.VII.C.S8	Establish and maintain a pitch attitude that transfers the weight of the airplane from the wheels to the wings as rapidly as possible.
AI.VII.C.S9	Lift off at the lowest possible airspeed and remain in ground effect while accelerating to V_X or V_Y, as appropriate.
AI.VII.C.S10	Establish a pitch attitude for V_X or V_Y, as appropriate, and maintain selected airspeed ±5 knots during the climb.
AI.VII.C.S11	Configure the airplane after a positive rate of climb has been verified or in accordance with airplane manufacturer's instructions.
AI.VII.C.S12	Maintain V_X or V_Y, as appropriate, ±5 knots to a safe maneuvering altitude.

AI.VII.C.S13	Maintain directional control and proper wind-drift correction throughout takeoff and climb.
AI.VII.C.S14	Comply with noise abatement procedures, as applicable.
AI.VII.C.S15	Analyze and correct common errors related to this Task.

Task D. Soft-Field Approach and Landing (ASEL)

References: *AIM; FAA-H-8083-2, FAA-H-8083-3, FAA-H-8083-9, FAA-H-8083-25; POH/AFM*

Objective: To determine the applicant understands soft-field approach and landing, can apply that knowledge, manage associated risks, demonstrate appropriate skills, and provide effective instruction.

Knowledge:	The applicant demonstrates instructional knowledge by describing and explaining:
AI.VII.D.K1	Purpose of and procedures for soft-field approach and landing.
AI.VII.D.K2	A stabilized approach, including energy management concepts.
AI.VII.D.K3	Effects of atmospheric conditions, including wind, on approach and landing performance.
AI.VII.D.K4	Wind correction techniques on approach and landing.
AI.VII.D.K5	Common errors related to this Task.

Risk Management:	The applicant explains and teaches how to identify and manage risk associated with:
AI.VII.D.R1	Selection of runway based on pilot capability, airplane performance and limitations, available distance, and wind.
AI.VII.D.R2	Effects of:
AI.VII.D.R2a	a. Crosswind
AI.VII.D.R2b	b. Windshear
AI.VII.D.R2c	c. Tailwind
AI.VII.D.R2d	d. Wake turbulence
AI.VII.D.R2e	e. Runway surface/condition
AI.VII.D.R3	Planning for:
AI.VII.D.R3a	a. Rejected landing and go-around
AI.VII.D.R3b	b. Land and hold short operations (LAHSO)
AI.VII.D.R4	Collision hazards.
AI.VII.D.R5	Low altitude maneuvering, including stall, spin, or controlled flight into terrain (CFIT).
AI.VII.D.R6	Distractions, task prioritization, loss of situational awareness, or disorientation.

Skills:	The applicant demonstrates and simultaneously explains how to:
AI.VII.D.S1	Complete the appropriate checklist(s).
AI.VII.D.S2	Make radio calls as appropriate.
AI.VII.D.S3	Ensure the airplane is aligned with the correct/assigned runway.
AI.VII.D.S4	Scan the landing runway and adjoining area for traffic and obstructions.
AI.VII.D.S5	Select and aim for a suitable touchdown point considering the wind conditions, landing surface, and obstructions.

AI.VII.D.S6	Establish the recommended approach and landing configuration, airspeed, and trim, and adjust pitch attitude and power as required to maintain a stabilized approach.
AI.VII.D.S7	Maintain manufacturer's published approach airspeed or in its absence not more than 1.3 times the stalling speed or the minimum steady flight speed in the landing configuration (V_{SO}), ±5 knots with gust factor applied.
AI.VII.D.S8	Maintain directional control and appropriate crosswind correction throughout the approach and landing.
AI.VII.D.S9	Make smooth, timely, and correct control inputs during the round out and touchdown, and, for tricycle gear airplanes, keep the nose wheel off the surface until loss of elevator effectiveness.
AI.VII.D.S10	Touch down at a proper pitch attitude with minimum sink rate, no side drift, and with the airplane's longitudinal axis aligned with the center of the runway.
AI.VII.D.S11	Maintain elevator as recommended by manufacturer during rollout and exit the "soft" area at a speed that would preclude sinking into the surface.
AI.VII.D.S12	Execute a timely go-around if the approach cannot be made within the tolerances specified above or for any other condition that may result in an unsafe approach or landing.
AI.VII.D.S13	Maintain proper position of the flight controls and sufficient speed to taxi while on the soft surface.
AI.VII.D.S14	Analyze and correct common errors related to this Task.

Task E. Short-Field Takeoff and Maximum Performance Climb (ASEL, AMEL)

References: AIM; FAA-H-8083-2, FAA-H-8083-3, FAA-H-8083-9, FAA-H-8083-25; POH/AFM

Objective: To determine the applicant understands short-field takeoff and maximum performance climb, can apply that knowledge, manage associated risks, demonstrate appropriate skills, and provide effective instruction.

Knowledge: The applicant demonstrates instructional knowledge by describing and explaining:

AI.VII.E.K1	Purpose of and procedures for short-field takeoff and maximum performance climb.
AI.VII.E.K2	Effects of atmospheric conditions, including wind, on takeoff and climb performance.
AI.VII.E.K3	Best angle of climb speed (V_X) and best rate of climb speed (V_Y).
AI.VII.E.K4	Appropriate airplane configuration.
AI.VII.E.K5	Common errors related to this Task.

Risk Management: The applicant explains and teaches how to identify and manage risk associated with:

AI.VII.E.R1	Selection of runway based on pilot capability, airplane performance and limitations, available distance, and wind.
AI.VII.E.R2	Effects of:
AI.VII.E.R2a	a. Crosswind
AI.VII.E.R2b	b. Windshear
AI.VII.E.R2c	c. Tailwind
AI.VII.E.R2d	d. Wake turbulence
AI.VII.E.R2e	e. Landing surface/condition

AI.VII.E.R3	Abnormal operations, including planning for:
AI.VII.E.R3a	a. Rejected takeoff
AI.VII.E.R3b	b. Potential engine failure in takeoff/climb phase of flight
AI.VII.E.R4	Collision hazards.
AI.VII.E.R5	Low altitude maneuvering, including stall, spin, or controlled flight into terrain (CFIT).
AI.VII.E.R6	Distractions, task prioritization, loss of situational awareness, or disorientation.

Skills:	The applicant demonstrates and simultaneously explains how to:
AI.VII.E.S1	Complete the appropriate checklist(s).
AI.VII.E.S2	Make radio calls as appropriate.
AI.VII.E.S3	Verify assigned/correct runway.
AI.VII.E.S4	Determine wind direction with or without visible wind direction indicators.
AI.VII.E.S5	Position the flight controls for the existing wind, if applicable.
AI.VII.E.S6	Clear the area, taxi into takeoff position, and align the airplane on the runway centerline utilizing maximum available takeoff area.
AI.VII.E.S7	Apply brakes while setting engine power to achieve maximum performance.
AI.VII.E.S8	Confirm takeoff power prior to brake release and verify proper engine and flight instrument indications prior to rotation.
AI.VII.E.S9	Rotate and lift off at the recommended airspeed and accelerate to the recommended obstacle clearance airspeed or V_X, ±5 knots.
AI.VII.E.S10	Establish a pitch attitude to maintain the recommended obstacle clearance airspeed or V_X, ±5 knots until the obstacle is cleared or until the airplane is 50 feet above the surface.
AI.VII.E.S11	Establish a pitch attitude for V_Y and accelerate to V_Y ±5 knots after clearing the obstacle or at 50 feet above ground level (AGL) if simulating an obstacle.
AI.VII.E.S12	Configure the airplane in accordance with the manufacturer's guidance after a positive rate of climb has been verified.
AI.VII.E.S13	Maintain V_Y ±5 knots to a safe maneuvering altitude.
AI.VII.E.S14	Maintain directional control and proper wind-drift correction throughout takeoff and climb.
AI.VII.E.S15	Comply with noise abatement procedures, as applicable.
AI.VII.E.S16	Analyze and correct common errors related to this Task.

Task F. Short-Field Approach and Landing (ASEL, AMEL)

References: AIM; FAA-H-8083-2, FAA-H-8083-3, FAA-H-8083-9, FAA-H-8083-25; POH/AFM

Objective: To determine the applicant understands short-field approach and landing, can apply that knowledge, manage associated risks, demonstrate appropriate skills, and provide effective instruction.

Knowledge:	The applicant demonstrates instructional knowledge by describing and explaining:
AI.VII.F.K1	Purpose of and procedures for short-field approach and landing.
AI.VII.F.K2	A stabilized approach, including energy management concepts.
AI.VII.F.K3	Effects of atmospheric conditions, including wind, on approach and landing performance.

| AI.VII.F.K4 | Wind correction techniques on approach and landing. |
| AI.VII.F.K5 | Common errors related to this Task. |

Risk Management: The applicant explains and teaches how to identify and manage risk associated with:

AI.VII.F.R1	Selection of runway based on pilot capability, airplane performance and limitations, available distance, and wind.
AI.VII.F.R2	Effects of:
AI.VII.F.R2a	a. Crosswind
AI.VII.F.R2b	b. Windshear
AI.VII.F.R2c	c. Tailwind
AI.VII.F.R2d	d. Wake turbulence
AI.VII.F.R2e	e. Landing surface/condition
AI.VII.F.R3	Planning for:
AI.VII.F.R3a	a. Rejected landing and go-around
AI.VII.F.R3b	b. Land and hold short operations (LAHSO)
AI.VII.F.R4	Collision hazards.
AI.VII.F.R5	Low altitude maneuvering, including stall, spin, or controlled flight into terrain (CFIT).
AI.VII.F.R6	Distractions, task prioritization, loss of situational awareness, or disorientation.

Skills: The applicant demonstrates and simultaneously explains how to:

AI.VII.F.S1	Complete the appropriate checklist(s).
AI.VII.F.S2	Make radio calls as appropriate.
AI.VII.F.S3	Ensure the airplane is aligned with the correct/assigned runway.
AI.VII.F.S4	Scan the landing runway and adjoining area for traffic and obstructions.
AI.VII.F.S5	Select and aim for a suitable touchdown point considering the wind conditions, landing surface, and obstructions.
AI.VII.F.S6	Establish the recommended approach and landing configuration, airspeed, and trim, and adjust pitch attitude and power as required to maintain a stabilized approach.
AI.VII.F.S7	Maintain manufacturer's published approach airspeed or in its absence not more than 1.3 times the stalling speed or the minimum steady flight speed in the landing configuration (V_{SO}), ±5 knots with gust factor applied.
AI.VII.F.S8	Maintain directional control and appropriate crosswind correction throughout the approach and landing.
AI.VII.F.S9	Make smooth, timely, and correct control application before, during, and after touchdown.
AI.VII.F.S10	Touch down at a proper pitch attitude within 100 feet beyond or on the specified point, threshold markings, or runway numbers, with no side drift, minimum float, and with the airplane's longitudinal axis aligned with and over the runway centerline.
AI.VII.F.S11	Use manufacturer's recommended procedures for airplane configuration and braking.
AI.VII.F.S12	Execute a timely go-around if the approach cannot be made within the tolerances specified above or for any other condition that may result in an unsafe approach or landing.
AI.VII.F.S13	Analyze and correct common errors related to this Task.

Task G. Confined Area Takeoff and Maximum Performance Climb (ASES, AMES)

References: AIM; FAA-H-8083-2, FAA-H-8083-3, FAA-H-8083-9, FAA-H-8083-23, FAA-H-8083-25; POH/AFM

Objective: To determine the applicant understands confined area takeoff and maximum performance climb, can apply that knowledge, manage associated risks, demonstrate appropriate skills, and provide effective instruction.

Knowledge:	The applicant demonstrates instructional knowledge by describing and explaining:
AI.VII.G.K1	Purpose of and procedures for confined area takeoff and maximum performance climb.
AI.VII.G.K2	Effects of atmospheric conditions, including wind, on takeoff and climb performance.
AI.VII.G.K3	Best angle of climb speed (V_X) and best rate of climb speed (V_Y).
AI.VII.G.K4	Appropriate airplane configuration.
AI.VII.G.K5	Effects of water surface.
AI.VII.G.K6	Common errors related to this Task.

Risk Management:	The applicant explains and teaches how to identify and manage risk associated with:
AI.VII.G.R1	Selection of takeoff path based on pilot capability, airplane performance and limitations, available distance, and wind.
AI.VII.G.R2	Effects of:
AI.VII.G.R2a	a. Crosswind
AI.VII.G.R2b	b. Windshear
AI.VII.G.R2c	c. Tailwind
AI.VII.G.R2d	d. Wake turbulence
AI.VII.G.R2e	e. Water surface/condition
AI.VII.G.R3	Abnormal operations, including planning for:
AI.VII.G.R3a	a. Rejected takeoff
AI.VII.G.R3b	b. Potential engine failure in takeoff/climb phase of flight
AI.VII.G.R4	Collision hazards.
AI.VII.G.R5	Low altitude maneuvering, including stall, spin, or controlled flight into terrain (CFIT).
AI.VII.G.R6	Distractions, task prioritization, loss of situational awareness, or disorientation.

Skills:	The applicant demonstrates and simultaneously explains how to:
AI.VII.G.S1	Complete the appropriate checklist(s).
AI.VII.G.S2	Make radio calls as appropriate.
AI.VII.G.S3	Verify assigned/correct takeoff path.
AI.VII.G.S4	Determine wind direction with or without visible wind direction indicators.
AI.VII.G.S5	Position the flight controls for the existing wind, if applicable.
AI.VII.G.S6	Clear the area, taxi into takeoff position utilizing maximum available takeoff area, and align the airplane on the takeoff path.
AI.VII.G.S7	Retract the water rudders, as appropriate.

AI.VII.G.S8	Establish a pitch attitude that maintains the most efficient planing/lift-off attitude and correct for porpoising and skipping.
AI.VII.G.S9	Advance the throttle smoothly to takeoff power and confirm proper engine and flight instrument indications prior to rotation.
AI.VII.G.S10	Avoid excessive water spray on the propeller(s).
AI.VII.G.S11	Rotate and lift off at the recommended airspeed, and accelerate to the recommended obstacle clearance airspeed or V_X.
AI.VII.G.S12	Establish a pitch attitude to maintain the recommended obstacle clearance airspeed or V_X, ±5 knots until the obstacle is cleared or until the airplane is 50 feet above the surface.
AI.VII.G.S13	Establish a pitch attitude for V_Y and accelerate to V_Y ±5 knots after clearing the obstacle or at 50 feet above ground level (AGL) if simulating an obstacle.
AI.VII.G.S14	Retract flaps, if extended, after a positive rate of climb has been verified or in accordance with airplane manufacturer's guidance.
AI.VII.G.S15	Maintain V_Y ±5 knots to a safe maneuvering altitude.
AI.VII.G.S16	Maintain directional control and proper wind-drift correction throughout takeoff and climb.
AI.VII.G.S17	Comply with noise abatement procedures, as applicable.
AI.VII.G.S18	Analyze and correct common errors related to this Task.

Task H. Confined Area Approach and Landing (ASES, AMES)

References: AIM; FAA-H-8083-2, FAA-H-8083-3, FAA-H-8083-9, FAA-H-8083-23, FAA-H-8083-25; POH/AFM

Objective: To determine the applicant understands confined area approach and landing, can apply that knowledge, manage associated risks, demonstrate appropriate skills, and provide effective instruction.

Knowledge:	The applicant demonstrates instructional knowledge by describing and explaining:
AI.VII.H.K1	Purpose of and procedures for confined area approach and landing.
AI.VII.H.K2	A stabilized approach, including energy management concepts.
AI.VII.H.K3	Effects of atmospheric conditions, including wind, on approach and landing performance.
AI.VII.H.K4	Wind correction techniques on approach and landing.
AI.VII.H.K5	Common errors related to this Task.

Risk Management:	The applicant explains and teaches how to identify and manage risk associated with:
AI.VII.H.R1	Selection of approach path and touchdown area based on pilot capability, airplane performance and limitations, available distance, and wind.
AI.VII.H.R2	Effects of:
AI.VII.H.R2a	a. Crosswind
AI.VII.H.R2b	b. Windshear
AI.VII.H.R2c	c. Tailwind
AI.VII.H.R2d	d. Wake turbulence
AI.VII.H.R2e	e. Water surface/condition
AI.VII.H.R3	Planning for a go-around and rejected landing.

AI.VII.H.R4	Collision hazards.
AI.VII.H.R5	Low altitude maneuvering, including stall, spin, or controlled flight into terrain (CFIT).
AI.VII.H.R6	Distractions, task prioritization, loss of situational awareness, or disorientation.

Skills:	The applicant demonstrates and simultaneously explains how to:
AI.VII.H.S1	Complete the appropriate checklist(s).
AI.VII.H.S2	Make radio calls as appropriate.
AI.VII.H.S3	Ensure the airplane is aligned for an approach to the correct/assigned landing surface.
AI.VII.H.S4	Scan the landing area for traffic and obstructions.
AI.VII.H.S5	Select and aim for a suitable touchdown point considering the wind conditions, landing surface, and obstructions.
AI.VII.H.S6	Establish the recommended approach and landing configuration, airspeed, and trim, and adjust pitch attitude and power as required to maintain a stabilized approach.
AI.VII.H.S7	Maintain manufacturer's published approach airspeed or in its absence not more than 1.3 V_{SO}, +10/-5 knots with gust factor applied.
AI.VII.H.S8	Maintain directional control and appropriate crosswind correction throughout the approach and landing.
AI.VII.H.S9	Make smooth, timely, and correct control application before, during, and after touchdown.
AI.VII.H.S10	Contact the water at the recommended airspeed with a proper pitch attitude for the surface conditions.
AI.VII.H.S11	Touch down at a proper pitch attitude, within 100 feet beyond or on the specified point, with no side drift, minimum float, and with the airplane's longitudinal axis aligned with the projected landing path.
AI.VII.H.S12	Execute a timely go-around if the approach cannot be made within the tolerances specified above or for any other condition that may result in an unsafe approach or landing.
AI.VII.H.S13	Apply elevator control as necessary to stop in the shortest distance consistent with safety.
AI.VII.H.S14	Analyze and correct common errors related to this Task.

Task I. Glassy Water Takeoff and Climb (ASES, AMES)

References: AIM; FAA-H-8083-2, FAA-H-8083-9, FAA-H-8083-23, FAA-H-8083-25; POH/AFM

Objective: To determine the applicant understands glassy-water takeoff and climb, can apply that knowledge, manage associated risks, demonstrate appropriate skills, and provide effective instruction.

Note: If a glassy water condition does not exist, the applicant must be evaluated by simulating the Task.

Knowledge:	The applicant demonstrates instructional knowledge by describing and explaining:
AI.VII.I.K1	Purpose of and procedures for glassy water takeoff and climb.
AI.VII.I.K2	Effects of atmospheric conditions, including wind, on takeoff and climb performance.
AI.VII.I.K3	Best angle of climb speed (V_X) and best rate of climb speed (V_Y).
AI.VII.I.K4	Appropriate airplane configuration.
AI.VII.I.K5	Appropriate use of glassy water takeoff and climb technique.
AI.VII.I.K6	Common errors related to this Task.

Risk Management: The applicant explains and teaches how to identify and manage risk associated with:

AI.VII.I.R1	Selection of takeoff path based on pilot capability, airplane performance and limitations, and available distance.
AI.VII.I.R2	Water surface/condition.
AI.VII.I.R3	Abnormal operations, including planning for:
AI.VII.I.R3a	a. Rejected takeoff
AI.VII.I.R3b	b. Potential engine failure in takeoff/climb phase of flight
AI.VII.I.R4	Collision hazards.
AI.VII.I.R5	Low altitude maneuvering, including stall, spin, or controlled flight into terrain (CFIT).
AI.VII.I.R6	Distractions, task prioritization, loss of situational awareness, or disorientation.
AI.VII.I.R7	Gear position in an amphibious airplane.

Skills: The applicant demonstrates and simultaneously explains how to:

AI.VII.I.S1	Complete the appropriate checklist(s).
AI.VII.I.S2	Make radio calls as appropriate.
AI.VII.I.S3	Position flight controls and configure the aircraft for the existing conditions.
AI.VII.I.S4	Clear the area, select appropriate takeoff path considering surface hazards or vessels and surface conditions.
AI.VII.I.S5	Retract the water rudders, as appropriate.
AI.VII.I.S6	Advance the throttle smoothly to takeoff power and confirm proper engine and flight instrument indications prior to rotation.
AI.VII.I.S7	Establish and maintain an appropriate planing attitude, directional control, and correct for porpoising, skipping, and increase in water drag.
AI.VII.I.S8	Avoid excessive water spray on the propeller(s).
AI.VII.I.S9	Use appropriate techniques to lift seaplane from the water considering surface conditions.
AI.VII.I.S10	Establish proper attitude/airspeed and accelerate to V_Y ±5 knots during the climb.
AI.VII.I.S11	Configure the airplane after a positive rate of climb has been verified or in accordance with airplane manufacturer's instructions.
AI.VII.I.S12	Maintain V_Y ±5 knots to a safe maneuvering altitude.
AI.VII.I.S13	Maintain directional control throughout takeoff and climb.
AI.VII.I.S14	Analyze and correct common errors related to this Task.

Task J. Glassy Water Approach and Landing (ASES, AMES)

References: *AIM; FAA-H-8083-2, FAA-H-8083-9, FAA-H-8083-23, FAA-H-8083-25; POH/AFM*

Objective: To determine the applicant understands glassy-water approach and landing, can apply that knowledge, manage associated risks, demonstrate appropriate skills, and provide effective instruction.

Note: *If a glassy water condition does not exist, the applicant must be evaluated by simulating the Task.*

Knowledge:	The applicant demonstrates instructional knowledge by describing and explaining:
AI.VII.J.K1	Purpose of and procedures for glassy water approach and landing.
AI.VII.J.K2	A stabilized approach, including energy management concepts.
AI.VII.J.K3	Effects of atmospheric conditions, including wind, on approach and landing performance.
AI.VII.J.K4	When and why glassy water techniques are used.
AI.VII.J.K5	Common errors related to this Task.

Risk Management:	The applicant explains and teaches how to identify and manage risk associated with:
AI.VII.J.R1	Selection of approach path and touchdown area based on pilot capability, airplane performance and limitations, and available distance.
AI.VII.J.R2	Water surface/condition.
AI.VII.J.R3	Planning for a go-around and rejected landing.
AI.VII.J.R4	Collision hazards.
AI.VII.J.R5	Low altitude maneuvering, including stall, spin, or controlled flight into terrain (CFIT).
AI.VII.J.R6	Distractions, task prioritization, loss of situational awareness, or disorientation.
AI.VII.J.R7	Gear position in an amphibious airplane.

Skills:	The applicant demonstrates and simultaneously explains how to:
AI.VII.J.S1	Complete the appropriate checklist(s).
AI.VII.J.S2	Make radio calls as appropriate.
AI.VII.J.S3	Scan the landing area for traffic and obstructions.
AI.VII.J.S4	Select a proper approach and landing path considering the landing surface, visual attitude references, water depth, and collision hazards.
AI.VII.J.S5	Establish the recommended approach and landing configuration, airspeed, and trim, and adjust pitch attitude and power as required to maintain a stabilized approach.
AI.VII.J.S6	Maintain manufacturer's published approach airspeed or in its absence not more than 1.3 V_{SO}, ±5 knots.
AI.VII.J.S7	Make smooth, timely, and correct power and control adjustments to maintain proper pitch attitude and rate of descent to touchdown.
AI.VII.J.S8	Contact the water in a proper pitch attitude, and slow to idle taxi speed.
AI.VII.J.S9	Maintain directional control throughout the approach and landing.
AI.VII.J.S10	Analyze and correct common errors related to this Task.

Task K. Rough Water Takeoff and Climb (ASES, AMES)

References: AIM; FAA-H-8083-2, FAA-H-8083-9, FAA-H-8083-23, FAA-H-8083-25; POH/AFM

Objective: To determine the applicant understands rough water takeoff and climb, can apply that knowledge, manage associated risks, demonstrate appropriate skills, and provide effective instruction.

Note: If a rough water condition does not exist, the applicant must be evaluated by simulating the Task.

Knowledge:	The applicant demonstrates instructional knowledge by describing and explaining:

AI.VII.K.K1	Purpose of and procedures for a rough water takeoff and climb.
AI.VII.K.K2	Effects of atmospheric conditions, including wind, on takeoff and climb performance.
AI.VII.K.K3	Best angle of climb speed (V_X) and best rate of climb speed (V_Y).
AI.VII.K.K4	Appropriate airplane configuration.
AI.VII.K.K5	Appropriate use of rough water takeoff and climb technique.
AI.VII.K.K6	Common errors related to this Task.

Risk Management:	The applicant explains and teaches how to identify and manage risk associated with:
AI.VII.K.R1	Selection of takeoff path based on pilot capability, airplane performance and limitations, available distance, and wind.
AI.VII.K.R2	Effects of:
AI.VII.K.R2a	a. Crosswind
AI.VII.K.R2b	b. Windshear
AI.VII.K.R2c	c. Tailwind
AI.VII.K.R2d	d. Wake turbulence
AI.VII.K.R2e	e. Water surface/condition
AI.VII.K.R3	Abnormal operations, including planning for:
AI.VII.K.R3a	a. Rejected takeoff
AI.VII.K.R3b	b. Potential engine failure in takeoff/climb phase of flight
AI.VII.K.R4	Collision hazards.
AI.VII.K.R5	Low altitude maneuvering, including stall, spin, or controlled flight into terrain (CFIT).
AI.VII.K.R6	Distractions, task prioritization, loss of situational awareness, or disorientation.
AI.VII.K.R7	Gear position in an amphibious airplane.

Skills:	The applicant demonstrates and simultaneously explains how to:
AI.VII.K.S1	Complete the appropriate checklist(s).
AI.VII.K.S2	Make radio calls as appropriate.
AI.VII.K.S3	Verify assigned/correct takeoff path.
AI.VII.K.S4	Determine wind direction with or without visible wind direction indicators.
AI.VII.K.S5	Position flight controls and configure the airplane for the existing conditions.
AI.VII.K.S6	Clear the area, select an appropriate takeoff path considering wind, swells, surface hazards, or vessels.
AI.VII.K.S7	Retract the water rudders, as appropriate.
AI.VII.K.S8	Advance the throttle smoothly to takeoff power and confirm proper engine and flight instrument indications prior to rotation.
AI.VII.K.S9	Establish and maintain an appropriate planing attitude, directional control, and correct for porpoising, skipping, and increase in water drag.
AI.VII.K.S10	Avoid excessive water spray on the propeller(s).
AI.VII.K.S11	Lift off at minimum airspeed and accelerate to V_Y ±5 knots before leaving ground effect.

AI.VII.K.S12	Configure the airplane after a positive rate of climb has been verified or in accordance with airplane manufacturer's instructions.
AI.VII.K.S13	Maintain V_Y ±5 knots to a safe maneuvering altitude.
AI.VII.K.S14	Maintain directional control and proper wind-drift correction throughout takeoff and climb.
AI.VII.K.S15	Analyze and correct common errors related to this Task.

Task L. Rough Water Approach and Landing (ASES, AMES)

References: AIM; FAA-H-8083-2, FAA-H-8083-9, FAA-H-8083-23, FAA-H-8083-25; POH/AFM

Objective: To determine the applicant understands rough water approach, can apply that knowledge, manage associated risks, demonstrate appropriate skills, and provide effective instruction.

Note: If a rough water condition does not exist, the applicant must be evaluated by simulating the Task.

Knowledge:	The applicant demonstrates instructional knowledge by describing and explaining:
AI.VII.L.K1	Purpose of and procedures for rough water approach and landing.
AI.VII.L.K2	A stabilized approach, including energy management concepts.
AI.VII.L.K3	Effects of atmospheric conditions, including wind, on approach and landing performance.
AI.VII.L.K4	Wind correction techniques on approach and landing.
AI.VII.L.K5	When and why rough water techniques are used.
AI.VII.L.K6	Common errors related to this Task.

Risk Management:	The applicant explains and teaches how to identify and manage risk associated with:
AI.VII.L.R1	Selection of approach path and touchdown area based on pilot capability, airplane performance and limitations, available distance, and wind.
AI.VII.L.R2	Effects of:
AI.VII.L.R2a	a. Crosswind
AI.VII.L.R2b	b. Windshear
AI.VII.L.R2c	c. Tailwind
AI.VII.L.R2d	d. Wake turbulence
AI.VII.L.R2e	e. Water surface/condition
AI.VII.L.R3	Planning for a go-around and rejected landing.
AI.VII.L.R4	Collision hazards.
AI.VII.L.R5	Low altitude maneuvering, including stall, spin, or controlled flight into terrain (CFIT).
AI.VII.L.R6	Distractions, task prioritization, loss of situational awareness, or disorientation.
AI.VII.L.R7	Gear position in an amphibious airplane.

Skills:	The applicant demonstrates and simultaneously explains how to:
AI.VII.L.S1	Complete the appropriate checklist(s).
AI.VII.L.S2	Make radio calls as appropriate.

AI.VII.L.S3	Ensure the airplane is aligned with the correct/assigned waterway.
AI.VII.L.S4	Scan the landing area for traffic and obstructions.
AI.VII.L.S5	Select and aim for a suitable touchdown point considering the wind conditions, landing surface, and obstructions.
AI.VII.L.S6	Establish the recommended approach and landing configuration, airspeed, and trim, and adjust pitch attitude and power as required to maintain a stabilized approach.
AI.VII.L.S7	Maintain manufacturer's published approach airspeed or in its absence not more than 1.3 times the stalling speed or the minimum steady flight speed in the landing configuration (V_{SO}), ±5 knots with gust factor applied.
AI.VII.L.S8	Maintain directional control and appropriate crosswind correction throughout the approach and landing.
AI.VII.L.S9	Make smooth, timely, and correct power and control adjustments to maintain proper pitch attitude and rate of descent to touchdown.
AI.VII.L.S10	Contact the water in a proper pitch attitude, considering the type of rough water.
AI.VII.L.S11	Analyze and correct common errors related to this Task.

Task M. Slip to a Landing (ASEL, ASES)

References: AIM; FAA-H-8083-2, FAA-H-8083-3, FAA-H-8083-9, FAA-H-8083-25; POH/AFM

Objective: To determine the applicant understands a slip to a landing, can apply that knowledge, manage associated risks, demonstrate appropriate skills, and provide effective instruction.

Knowledge:	The applicant demonstrates instructional knowledge by describing and explaining:
AI.VII.M.K1	Purpose of and procedures for forward or side slip to a landing.
AI.VII.M.K2	Concepts of energy management during a forward or side slip approach.
AI.VII.M.K3	Effects of atmospheric conditions, including wind, on approach and landing performance.
AI.VII.M.K4	Wind correction techniques during a forward or side slip.
AI.VII.M.K5	Common errors related to this Task.

Risk Management:	The applicant explains and teaches how to identify and manage risk associated with:
AI.VII.M.R1	Selection of runway/landing surface, approach path, and touchdown area based on pilot capability, aircraft performance and limitations, available distance, and wind.
AI.VII.M.R2	Effects of:
AI.VII.M.R2a	a. Crosswind
AI.VII.M.R2b	b. Windshear
AI.VII.M.R2c	c. Tailwind
AI.VII.M.R2d	d. Wake turbulence
AI.VII.M.R2e	e. Landing surface/condition
AI.VII.M.R3	Planning for:
AI.VII.M.R3a	a. Rejected landing and go-around
AI.VII.M.R3b	b. Land and hold short operations (LAHSO)

AI.VII.M.R4	Collision hazards.
AI.VII.M.R5	Low altitude maneuvering, including stall, spin, or controlled flight into terrain (CFIT).
AI.VII.M.R6	Distractions, task prioritization, loss of situational awareness, or disorientation.
AI.VII.M.R7	Forward slip operations, including fuel flowage, tail stalls with flaps, and airspeed control.
AI.VII.M.R8	Surface contact with the airplane's longitudinal axis misaligned.
AI.VII.M.R9	Unstable approach.

Skills:	The applicant demonstrates and simultaneously explains how to:
AI.VII.M.S1	Complete the appropriate checklist(s).
AI.VII.M.S2	Make radio calls as appropriate.
AI.VII.M.S3	Plan and follow a flightpath to the selected landing area considering altitude, wind, terrain, and obstructions.
AI.VII.M.S4	Select the most suitable touchdown point based on wind, landing surface, obstructions, and airplane limitations.
AI.VII.M.S5	Position airplane on downwind leg, parallel to landing runway or selected landing surface.
AI.VII.M.S6	Configure the airplane correctly.
AI.VII.M.S7	As necessary, correlate crosswind with direction of slip and transition to sideslip as appropriate before touchdown.
AI.VII.M.S8	Touch down at a proper pitch attitude, within 400 feet beyond or on the specified point, with no side drift, and with the airplane's longitudinal axis aligned with and over the runway center/landing path.
AI.VII.M.S9	Maintain a ground track aligned with the runway center/landing path.
AI.VII.M.S10	Analyze and correct common errors related to this Task.

Task N. Go-Around/Rejected Landing

References: AIM; FAA-H-8083-2, FAA-H-8083-3, FAA-H-8083-9, FAA-H-8083-23, FAA-H-8083-25; POH/AFM

Objective: To determine the applicant understands go-around/rejected landing with emphasis on factors that contribute to landing conditions that may require a go-around, can apply that knowledge, manage associated risks, demonstrate appropriate skills, and provide effective instruction.

Knowledge:	The applicant demonstrates instructional knowledge by describing and explaining:
AI.VII.N.K1	Purpose of and procedures for go-around or rejected landing.
AI.VII.N.K2	A stabilized approach, including energy management concepts.
AI.VII.N.K3	Effects of atmospheric conditions, including wind and density altitude, on a go-around or rejected landing.
AI.VII.N.K4	Wind correction techniques on takeoff/departure and approach/landing.
AI.VII.N.K5	Common errors related to this Task.

Risk Management:	The applicant explains and teaches how to identify and manage risk associated with:
AI.VII.N.R1	Delayed recognition of the need for a go-around/rejected landing.
AI.VII.N.R2	Delayed performance of a go-around at low altitude.

AI.VII.N.R3	Power application.
AI.VII.N.R4	Configuring the airplane.
AI.VII.N.R5	Collision hazards.
AI.VII.N.R6	Low altitude maneuvering, including stall, spin, or controlled flight into terrain (CFIT).
AI.VII.N.R7	Distractions, task prioritization, loss of situational awareness, or disorientation.
AI.VII.N.R8	Managing a go-around/rejected landing after accepting a LAHSO clearance.
AI.VII.N.R9	Runway incursion.

Skills:	The applicant demonstrates and simultaneously explains how to:
AI.VII.N.S1	Complete the appropriate checklist(s).
AI.VII.N.S2	Make radio calls as appropriate.
AI.VII.N.S3	Make a timely decision to discontinue the approach to landing.
AI.VII.N.S4	Apply takeoff power immediately and transition to climb pitch attitude for V_X or V_Y as appropriate ±5 knots.
AI.VII.N.S5	Configure the airplane after a positive rate of climb has been verified or in accordance with airplane manufacturer's instructions.
AI.VII.N.S6	Maneuver to the side of the runway/landing area when necessary to clear and avoid conflicting traffic.
AI.VII.N.S7	Maintain V_Y ±5 knots to a safe maneuvering altitude.
AI.VII.N.S8	Maintain directional control and proper wind-drift correction throughout the climb.
AI.VII.N.S9	Analyze and correct common errors related to this Task.

Task O. Power-Off 180° Accuracy Approach and Landing (ASEL, ASES)

References:	AIM; FAA-H-8083-2, FAA-H-8083-3, FAA-H-8083-9, FAA-H-8083-25; POH/AFM
Objective:	To determine the applicant understands a power-off 180° accuracy approach, can apply that knowledge, manage associated risks, demonstrate appropriate skills, and provide effective instruction.
Note:	See Appendix 3: Aircraft, Equipment, and Operational Requirements & Limitations for information related to this Task.

Knowledge:	The applicant demonstrates instructional knowledge by describing and explaining:
AI.VII.O.K1	Purpose of and procedures for proper 180° accuracy approach and landing.
AI.VII.O.K2	A stabilized approach, including energy management concepts.
AI.VII.O.K3	Effects of atmospheric conditions, including wind, on approach and landing.
AI.VII.O.K4	Wind correction techniques on approach and landing.
AI.VII.O.K5	Common errors related to this Task.

Risk Management:	The applicant explains and teaches how to identify and manage risk associated with:
AI.VII.O.R1	Selection of runway/landing surface, approach path, and touchdown area based on pilot capability, aircraft performance and limitations, available distance, and wind.

AI.VII.O.R2	Effects of:
AI.VII.O.R2a	a. Crosswind
AI.VII.O.R2b	b. Windshear
AI.VII.O.R2c	c. Tailwind
AI.VII.O.R2d	d. Wake turbulence
AI.VII.O.R2e	e. Landing surface/condition
AI.VII.O.R3	Planning for:
AI.VII.O.R3a	a. Rejected landing and go-around
AI.VII.O.R3b	b. Land and hold short operations (LAHSO)
AI.VII.O.R4	Collision hazards.
AI.VII.O.R5	Low altitude maneuvering, including stall, spin, or controlled flight into terrain (CFIT).
AI.VII.O.R6	Distractions, task prioritization, loss of situational awareness, or disorientation.
AI.VII.O.R7	Forward slip operations, including fuel flowage, tail stalls with flaps, and airspeed control.

Skills:	The applicant demonstrates and simultaneously explains how to:
AI.VII.O.S1	Complete the appropriate checklist(s).
AI.VII.O.S2	Make radio calls as appropriate.
AI.VII.O.S3	Plan and follow a flightpath to the selected landing area considering altitude, wind, terrain, and obstructions.
AI.VII.O.S4	Select the most suitable touchdown point based on wind, landing surface, obstructions, and aircraft limitations.
AI.VII.O.S5	Position airplane on downwind leg, parallel to landing runway.
AI.VII.O.S6	Correctly configure the airplane.
AI.VII.O.S7	As necessary, correlate crosswind with direction of forward slip and transition to side slip before touchdown.
AI.VII.O.S8	Touch down at a proper pitch attitude, within 200 feet beyond or on the specified point with no side drift and with the airplane's longitudinal axis aligned with and over the runway centerline or landing path, as applicable.
AI.VII.O.S9	Analyze and correct common errors related to this Task.

Area of Operation VIII. Fundamentals of Flight

Note: *The evaluator must select at least one Task from this Area of Operation.*

Task A. Straight-and-Level Flight

References: *FAA-H-8083-2, FAA-H-8083-3, FAA-H-8083-9, FAA-H-8083-25*

Objective: To determine the applicant understands straight-and-level flight, can apply that knowledge, manage associated risks, demonstrate appropriate skills, and provide effective instruction.

Knowledge:	The applicant demonstrates instructional knowledge by describing and explaining:
AI.VIII.A.K1	Purpose of and procedures for proper straight-and-level flight.
AI.VIII.A.K2	Flight control and trim use.
AI.VIII.A.K3	The pilot's visual references when performing the maneuver.
AI.VIII.A.K4	Integrated flight instruction.
AI.VIII.A.K5	Common errors related to this Task.

Risk Management:	The applicant explains and teaches how to identify and manage risk associated with:
AI.VIII.A.R1	Distractions, task prioritization, loss of situational awareness, or disorientation.
AI.VIII.A.R2	Collision hazards.

Skills:	The applicant demonstrates and simultaneously explains how to:
AI.VIII.A.S1	Establish and maintain straight-and-level flight.
AI.VIII.A.S2	Analyze and correct common errors related to this Task.

Task B. Level Turns

References: *FAA-H-8083-2, FAA-H-8083-3, FAA-H-8083-9, FAA-H-8083-25*

Objective: To determine the applicant understands level turns, can apply that knowledge, manage associated risks, demonstrate appropriate skills, and provide effective instruction.

Knowledge:	The applicant demonstrates instructional knowledge by describing and explaining:
AI.VIII.B.K1	Purpose of and procedures for level turns.
AI.VIII.B.K2	Flight control and trim use.
AI.VIII.B.K3	The pilot's visual references when performing the maneuver.
AI.VIII.B.K4	Integrated flight instruction.
AI.VIII.B.K5	Common errors related to this Task.

Risk Management:	The applicant explains and teaches how to identify and manage risk associated with:
AI.VIII.B.R1	Distractions, task prioritization, loss of situational awareness, or disorientation.
AI.VIII.B.R2	Collision hazards.

Skills:	The applicant demonstrates and simultaneously explains how to:
AI.VIII.B.S1	Establish, maintain, and roll out of a level turn.
AI.VIII.B.S2	Analyze and correct common errors related to this Task.

Task C. Straight Climbs and Climbing Turns

References: FAA-H-8083-2, FAA-H-8083-3, FAA-H-8083-9, FAA-H-8083-25

Objective: To determine the applicant understands straight climbs and climbing turns, can apply that knowledge, manage associated risks, demonstrate appropriate skills, and provide effective instruction.

Knowledge:	The applicant demonstrates instructional knowledge by describing and explaining:
AI.VIII.C.K1	Purpose of and procedures for straight climbs and climbing turns.
AI.VIII.C.K2	Flight control and trim use.
AI.VIII.C.K3	The pilot's visual references when performing the maneuver.
AI.VIII.C.K4	Integrated flight instruction.
AI.VIII.C.K5	Common errors related to this Task.

Risk Management:	The applicant explains and teaches how to identify and manage risk associated with:
AI.VIII.C.R1	Distractions, task prioritization, loss of situational awareness, or disorientation.
AI.VIII.C.R2	Collision hazards.

Skills:	The applicant demonstrates and simultaneously explains how to:
AI.VIII.C.S1	Establish, maintain, and level off from climbs and climbing turns.
AI.VIII.C.S2	Analyze and correct common errors related to this Task.

Task D. Straight Descents and Descending Turns

References: FAA-H-8083-2, FAA-H-8083-3, FAA-H-8083-9, FAA-H-8083-25

Objective: To determine the applicant understands straight descents and descending turns, can apply that knowledge, manage associated risks, demonstrate appropriate skills, and provide effective instruction.

Knowledge:	The applicant demonstrates instructional knowledge by describing and explaining:
AI.VIII.D.K1	Purpose of and procedures for straight descents and descending turns.
AI.VIII.D.K2	Flight control and trim use.
AI.VIII.D.K3	The pilot's visual references when performing the maneuver.
AI.VIII.D.K4	Integrated flight instruction.
AI.VIII.D.K5	Common errors related to this Task.

Risk
Management: The applicant explains and teaches how to identify and manage risk associated with:

AI.VIII.D.R1	Distractions, task prioritization, loss of situational awareness, or disorientation.
AI.VIII.D.R2	Collision hazards.

Skills: The applicant demonstrates and simultaneously explains how to:

AI.VIII.D.S1	Establish, maintain, and level off from straight descents and descending turns.
AI.VIII.D.S2	Analyze and correct common errors related to this Task.

Area of Operation IX. Performance and Ground Reference Maneuvers

Note: *For ASEL or ASES, the evaluator must select at least four Tasks including Task A or B, Task C or D, and Tasks E and F from Area of Operation IX , Performance and Ground Reference Maneuvers. For AMEL or AMES the evaluator must select at least Tasks A and E.*

Task A. Steep Turns

References: *FAA-H-8083-2, FAA-H-8083-3, FAA-H-8083-9, FAA-H-8083-25; POH/AFM*

Objective: To determine the applicant understands steep turns, can apply that knowledge, manage associated risks, demonstrate appropriate skills, and provide effective instruction.

Knowledge:	The applicant demonstrates instructional knowledge by describing and explaining:
AI.IX.A.K1	Purpose of and procedures for steep turn.
AI.IX.A.K2	Pilot sensations and control forces.
AI.IX.A.K3	Aerodynamics associated with steep turns, including:
AI.IX.A.K3a	a. Maintaining coordinated flight
AI.IX.A.K3b	b. Overbanking tendencies
AI.IX.A.K3c	c. Maneuvering speed, including the impact of weight changes
AI.IX.A.K3d	d. Load factor and accelerated stalls
AI.IX.A.K3e	e. Rate and radius of turn
AI.IX.A.K4	Common errors related to this Task.

Risk Management:	The applicant explains and teaches how to identify and manage risk associated with:
AI.IX.A.R1	Division of attention between aircraft control and orientation.
AI.IX.A.R2	Collision hazards.
AI.IX.A.R3	Low altitude maneuvering, including stall, spin, or controlled flight into terrain (CFIT).
AI.IX.A.R4	Distractions, task prioritization, loss of situational awareness, or disorientation.
AI.IX.A.R5	Uncoordinated flight.

Skills:	The applicant demonstrates and simultaneously explains how to:
AI.IX.A.S1	Clear the area.
AI.IX.A.S2	Establish the manufacturer's recommended airspeed; or if one is not available, an airspeed not to exceed maneuvering speed (VA).
AI.IX.A.S3	Roll into a coordinated 360° steep turn with approximately a 50° bank.
AI.IX.A.S4	Perform the Task in the opposite direction.
AI.IX.A.S5	Maintain the entry altitude ±100 feet, airspeed ±10 knots, bank ±5°, and roll out on the entry heading ±10°.
AI.IX.A.S6	Analyze and correct common errors related to this Task.

Task B. Steep Spiral (ASEL, ASES)

References: FAA-H-8083-2, FAA-H-8083-3, FAA-H-8083-9, FAA-H-8083-25; POH/AFM

Objective: To determine the applicant understands steep spirals, can apply that knowledge, manage associated risks, demonstrate appropriate skills, and provide effective instruction.

Knowledge:	The applicant demonstrates instructional knowledge by describing and explaining:
AI.IX.B.K1	Purpose of and procedures for a proper steep spiral.
AI.IX.B.K2	Relationship to emergency landing procedures.
AI.IX.B.K3	Maintaining a constant radius about a point.
AI.IX.B.K4	Effects of wind on ground track and relation to a ground reference.
AI.IX.B.K5	Common errors related to this Task.

Risk Management:	The applicant explains and teaches how to identify and manage risk associated with:
AI.IX.B.R1	Division of attention between aircraft control and orientation.
AI.IX.B.R2	Collision hazards.
AI.IX.B.R3	Low altitude maneuvering, including stall, spin, or controlled flight into terrain (CFIT).
AI.IX.B.R4	Distractions, task prioritization, loss of situational awareness, or disorientation.
AI.IX.B.R5	Uncoordinated flight.
AI.IX.B.R6	Effects of wind.
AI.IX.B.R7	Airframe or airspeed limitations.

Skills:	The applicant demonstrates and simultaneously explains how to:
AI.IX.B.S1	Clear the area.
AI.IX.B.S2	Select an altitude sufficient to continue through a series of at least three, 360° turns.
AI.IX.B.S3	Establish and maintain a steep spiral, not to exceed 60° angle of bank, to maintain a constant radius about a suitable ground reference point.
AI.IX.B.S4	Apply wind-drift correction to track a constant radius circle around selected reference point with bank not to exceed 60° a steepest point in turn.
AI.IX.B.S5	Divide attention between airplane control, traffic avoidance and the ground track while maintaining coordinated flight.
AI.IX.B.S6	Maintain the specified airspeed, ±10 knots and roll out toward an object or specified heading, ±10°, and complete the maneuver no lower than 1,500 feet above ground level (AGL).
AI.IX.B.S7	Analyze and correct common errors related to this Task.

Task C. Chandelles (ASEL, ASES)

References: FAA-H-8083-2, FAA-H-8083-3, FAA-H-8083-9, FAA-H-8083-25; POH/AFM

Objective: To determine the applicant understands chandelles, can apply that knowledge, manage associated risks, demonstrate appropriate skills, and provide effective instruction.

Knowledge:	The applicant demonstrates instructional knowledge by describing and explaining:
AI.IX.C.K1	Purpose of and procedures for chandelles.
AI.IX.C.K2	Aerodynamics associated with chandelles, including:
AI.IX.C.K2a	a. Maintaining coordinated flight
AI.IX.C.K2b	b. Overbanking tendencies
AI.IX.C.K2c	c. Maneuvering speed, including the impact of weight changes
AI.IX.C.K2d	d. Accelerated stalls
AI.IX.C.K3	Appropriate airplane configuration for maximum performance climb.
AI.IX.C.K4	Proper pitch control required for continuously decreasing airspeed.
AI.IX.C.K5	Common errors related to this Task.

Risk Management:	The applicant explains and teaches how to identify and manage risk associated with:
AI.IX.C.R1	Division of attention between aircraft control and orientation.
AI.IX.C.R2	Collision hazards.
AI.IX.C.R3	Low altitude maneuvering, including stall, spin, or controlled flight into terrain (CFIT).
AI.IX.C.R4	Distractions, task prioritization, loss of situational awareness, or disorientation.
AI.IX.C.R5	Uncoordinated flight.
AI.IX.C.R6	Energy management.
AI.IX.C.R7	Rate and radius of turn with confined area operations.

Skills:	The applicant demonstrates and simultaneously explains how to:
AI.IX.C.S1	Clear the area.
AI.IX.C.S2	Select an altitude that allows the maneuver to be performed no lower than 1,500 feet above ground level (AGL).
AI.IX.C.S3	Establish the appropriate entry configuration, power, and airspeed.
AI.IX.C.S4	Establish the angle of bank at approximately 30°.
AI.IX.C.S5	Simultaneously apply power and pitch to maintain a smooth, coordinated climbing turn, in either direction, to the 90° point, with a constant bank and continuously decreasing airspeed.
AI.IX.C.S6	Begin a coordinated constant rate rollout from the 90° point to the 180° point maintaining power and a constant pitch attitude.
AI.IX.C.S7	Complete rollout at the 180° point, ±10° just above a stall airspeed, and maintaining that airspeed momentarily avoiding a stall.
AI.IX.C.S8	Resume a straight-and-level flight with minimum loss of altitude.
AI.IX.C.S9	Analyze and correct common errors related to this Task.

Task D. Lazy Eights (ASEL, ASES)

References: FAA-H-8083-2, FAA-H-8083-3, FAA-H-8083-9, FAA-H-8083-25; POH/AFM

Objective: To determine the applicant understands lazy eights, can apply that knowledge, manage associated risks, demonstrate appropriate skills, and provide effective instruction.

Knowledge:	The applicant demonstrates instructional knowledge by describing and explaining:
AI.IX.D.K1	Purpose of and procedures for lazy eights.
AI.IX.D.K2	Aerodynamics associated with lazy eights, including how to maintain coordinated flight.
AI.IX.D.K3	Performance and airspeed limitations.
AI.IX.D.K4	Phases of the lazy eight maneuver from entry to recovery.
AI.IX.D.K5	Common errors related to this Task.

Risk Management:	The applicant explains and teaches how to identify and manage risk associated with:
AI.IX.D.R1	Division of attention between aircraft control and orientation.
AI.IX.D.R2	Collision hazards.
AI.IX.D.R3	Low altitude maneuvering, including stall, spin, or controlled flight into terrain (CFIT).
AI.IX.D.R4	Distractions, task prioritization, loss of situational awareness, or disorientation.
AI.IX.D.R5	Uncoordinated flight.
AI.IX.D.R6	Energy management.
AI.IX.D.R7	Accelerated stalls.

Skills:	The applicant demonstrates and simultaneously explains how to:
AI.IX.D.S1	Clear the area.
AI.IX.D.S2	Select an altitude that allows the maneuver to be performed no lower than 1,500 feet above ground level (AGL).
AI.IX.D.S3	Establish the recommended entry configuration, power, and airspeed.
AI.IX.D.S4	Maintain coordinated flight throughout the maneuver.
AI.IX.D.S5	Complete the maneuver in accordance with the following:
AI.IX.D.S5a	a. Approximately 30° bank at the steepest point
AI.IX.D.S5b	b. Constant change of pitch and roll rate and airspeed
AI.IX.D.S5c	c. Altitude at 180° point, ±100 feet from entry altitude
AI.IX.D.S5d	d. Airspeed at the 180° point, ±10 knots from entry airspeed
AI.IX.D.S5e	e. Heading at the 180° point, ±10°
AI.IX.D.S6	Continue the maneuver through the number of symmetrical loops specified, then resume straight-and-level flight.
AI.IX.D.S7	Analyze and correct common errors related to this Task.

Task E. Ground Reference Maneuvers

References: *FAA-H-8083-2, FAA-H-8083-3, FAA-H-8083-9, FAA-H-8083-25; POH/AFM*

Objective: To determine the applicant understands ground reference maneuvers, can apply that knowledge, manage associated risks, demonstrate appropriate skills, and provide effective instruction.

Note: *The evaluator selects at least one ground reference maneuver for the applicant to demonstrate.*

Knowledge:	The applicant demonstrates instructional knowledge by describing and explaining:
AI.IX.E.K1	Purpose of and procedures for ground reference maneuvers.
AI.IX.E.K2	Effects of wind on ground track and relation to a ground reference.
AI.IX.E.K3	Effects of bank angle and groundspeed on rate and radius of turn.
AI.IX.E.K4	Relationship of rectangular course to airport traffic pattern.
AI.IX.E.K5	Common errors related to this Task.

Risk Management:	The applicant explains and teaches how to identify and manage risk associated with:
AI.IX.E.R1	Division of attention between aircraft control and orientation.
AI.IX.E.R2	Collision hazards.
AI.IX.E.R3	Low altitude maneuvering, including stall, spin, or controlled flight into terrain (CFIT).
AI.IX.E.R4	Distractions, task prioritization, loss of situational awareness, or disorientation.
AI.IX.E.R5	Uncoordinated flight.

Skills:	The applicant demonstrates and simultaneously explains how to:
AI.IX.E.S1	Clear the area.
AI.IX.E.S2	Select a suitable ground reference area, line, or point as appropriate.
AI.IX.E.S3	Plan the maneuver:
AI.IX.E.S3a	a. Rectangular course: enter a left or right pattern, 600 to 1,000 feet above ground level (AGL) at an appropriate distance from the selected reference area, 45° to the downwind leg
AI.IX.E.S3b	b. S-turns: enter perpendicular to the selected reference line, 600 to 1,000 feet AGL at an appropriate distance from the selected reference area
AI.IX.E.S3c	c. Turns around a point: enter at an appropriate distance from the reference point, 600 to 1,000 feet AGL at an appropriate distance from the selected reference area
AI.IX.E.S4	Apply adequate wind-drift correction during straight and turning flight to maintain a constant ground track around a rectangular reference area, or to maintain a constant radius turn on each side of a selected reference line or point.
AI.IX.E.S5	If performing S-Turns, reverse the turn directly over the selected reference line; if performing turns around a point, complete turns in either direction, as specified by the evaluator.
AI.IX.E.S6	Divide attention between airplane control, traffic avoidance and the ground track while maintaining coordinated flight.
AI.IX.E.S7	Maintain altitude ±100 feet; maintain airspeed ±10 knots.
AI.IX.E.S8	Analyze and correct common errors related to this Task.

Task F. Eights on Pylons (ASEL, ASES)

References: *FAA-H-8083-2, FAA-H-8083-3, FAA-H-8083-9, FAA-H-8083-25; POH/AFM*

Objective: To determine the applicant understands eights on pylons, can apply that knowledge, manage associated risks, demonstrate appropriate skills, and provide effective instruction.

Knowledge:	The applicant demonstrates instructional knowledge by describing and explaining:
AI.IX.F.K1	Purpose of and procedures for eights on pylons.
AI.IX.F.K2	Aerodynamics associated with the eights on pylons, including coordinated and uncoordinated flight.
AI.IX.F.K3	Pivotal altitude and factors that affect it.
AI.IX.F.K4	Effect of wind on ground track.
AI.IX.F.K5	Phases of the eights on pylons maneuver from entry to recovery.
AI.IX.F.K6	Common errors related to this Task.

Risk Management:	The applicant explains and teaches how to identify and manage risk associated with:
AI.IX.F.R1	Division of attention between aircraft control and orientation.
AI.IX.F.R2	Collision hazards.
AI.IX.F.R3	Low altitude maneuvering, including stall, spin, or controlled flight into terrain (CFIT).
AI.IX.F.R4	Distractions, task prioritization, loss of situational awareness, or disorientation.
AI.IX.F.R5	Uncoordinated flight.
AI.IX.F.R6	Energy management.
AI.IX.F.R7	Emergency landing considerations.

Skills:	The applicant demonstrates and simultaneously explains how to:
AI.IX.F.S1	Clear the area.
AI.IX.F.S2	Determine the approximate pivotal altitude.
AI.IX.F.S3	Select suitable pylons that permits straight-and-level flight between the pylons.
AI.IX.F.S4	Enter the maneuver in the correct direction and position using an appropriate altitude and airspeed.
AI.IX.F.S5	Establish the correct bank angle for the conditions, not to exceed 40°.
AI.IX.F.S6	Apply smooth and continuous corrections so that the line-of-sight reference line remains on the pylon.
AI.IX.F.S7	Divide attention between accurate, coordinated airplane control and outside visual references.
AI.IX.F.S8	Maintain pylon position using appropriate pivotal altitude, avoiding slips and skids.
AI.IX.F.S9	Analyze and correct common errors related to this Task.

Area of Operation X. Slow Flight, Stalls, and Spins

Note: *For single-engine, the evaluator must select Task A or B; Task C, D, or E; Task F, G, or H; and Task I. For multiengine the evaluator must select Task A and Task C, D, or E.*

Task A. Maneuvering During Slow Flight

References: *AC 61-67; FAA-H-8083-2, FAA-H-8083-3, FAA-H-8083-9, FAA-H-8083-25; POH/AFM*

Objective: To determine the applicant understands maneuvering during slow flight in cruise configuration, can apply that knowledge, manage associated risks, demonstrate appropriate skills, and provide effective instruction.

Note: *See Appendix 2: Safety of Flight and Appendix 3: Aircraft, Equipment, and Operational Requirements & Limitations for information related to this Task.*

Knowledge:	The applicant demonstrates instructional knowledge by describing and explaining:
AI.X.A.K1	Purpose of and procedures for proper slow flight.
AI.X.A.K2	Aerodynamics associated with slow flight in various airplane configurations, including the relationship between angle of attack, airspeed, load factor, power setting, airplane weight and center of gravity, airplane attitude, and yaw effects.
AI.X.A.K3	Common errors related to this Task.

Risk Management:	The applicant explains and teaches how to identify and manage risk associated with:
AI.X.A.R1	Inadvertent slow flight and flight with a stall warning, which could lead to loss of control.
AI.X.A.R2	Range and limitations of stall warning indicators (e.g., aircraft buffet, stall horn, etc.).
AI.X.A.R3	Uncoordinated flight.
AI.X.A.R4	Effect of environmental elements on airplane performance (e.g., turbulence, microbursts, and high-density altitude).
AI.X.A.R5	Collision hazards.
AI.X.A.R6	Distractions, task prioritization, loss of situational awareness, or disorientation.

Skills:	The applicant demonstrates and simultaneously explains how to:
AI.X.A.S1	Clear the area.
AI.X.A.S2	Select an entry altitude that allows the Task to be completed no lower than 1,500 feet above ground level (AGL) (ASEL, ASES) or 3,000 feet AGL (AMEL, AMES).
AI.X.A.S3	Establish and maintain an airspeed at which any further increase in angle of attack, increase in load factor, or reduction in power, would result in a stall warning (e.g., aircraft buffet, stall horn, etc.).
AI.X.A.S4	Accomplish coordinated straight-and-level flight, turns, climbs, and descents with the aircraft configured as specified by the evaluator without a stall warning (e.g., aircraft buffet, stall horn, etc.).
AI.X.A.S5	Maintain the specified altitude, ±50 feet; specified heading, ±10°; airspeed, +5/-0 knots; and specified angle of bank, ±5°.
AI.X.A.S6	Analyze and correct common errors related to this Task.

Task B. Demonstration of Flight Characteristics at Various Configurations and Airspeeds (ASEL and ASES)

References: AC 61-67; FAA-H-8083-2, FAA-H-8083-3, FAA-H-8083-9, FAA-H-8083-25; POH/AFM

Objective: To determine the applicant understands flight characteristics and power required at different airspeeds and configurations appropriate to the make and model of airplane flown, can apply that knowledge, manage associated risks, demonstrate appropriate skills, and provide effective instruction.

Note: See Appendix 2: Safety of Flight and Appendix 3: Aircraft, Equipment, and Operational Requirements & Limitations for information related to this Task.

Knowledge:	The applicant demonstrates instructional knowledge by describing and explaining:
AI.X.B.K1	Purpose of and procedures for demonstration of flight characteristics at various configurations and airspeeds.
AI.X.B.K2	Power required at various airspeeds between cruise airspeed and critically slow airspeeds near the critical angle of attack.
AI.X.B.K3	The minimum power required speed and its role in differentiating the region of normal command and the region of reversed command on the power-required curve.
AI.X.B.K4	The relationships between lift, drag, angle of attack, airspeed, load factor, power required, weight, center of gravity, attitude, yaw effects, controllability, and stalls and spins.
AI.X.B.K5	Pitch, power, and trim control inputs that are required to operate the airplane in level flight, turns, climbs, and descents and how the control inputs change at various airspeeds between cruise airspeed and critically slow airspeeds.
AI.X.B.K6	Flight characteristics and aerodynamics associated with configuration changes applicable to the specific to the make and model of airplane provided for the practical test.
AI.X.B.K7	Airspeeds specific to the airplane for various operations, how to identify them on the airspeed indicator (if applicable), and their significance in airplane performance, including:
AI.X.B.K7a	a. Design/operating maneuvering speed
AI.X.B.K7b	b. Landing gear extended/operating speed, if applicable
AI.X.B.K7c	c. Flaps extended/operating speed, if applicable
AI.X.B.K7d	d. Best glide speed
AI.X.B.K7e	e. Reference landing speed
AI.X.B.K7f	f. Stalling speeds
AI.X.B.K8	Common errors related to this Task.

Risk Management:	The applicant explains and teaches how to identify and manage risk associated with:
AI.X.B.R1	Lack of familiarity with airplane airspeed limitations and interpretation of the airspeed indicator.
AI.X.B.R2	Exceeding airspeed limitations.
AI.X.B.R3	Flight characteristics in the region of reversed command and the potential for loss of control.
AI.X.B.R4	Inadvertent exceedance of the critical angle of attack.
AI.X.B.R5	Range, limitations, and operational characteristics of airspeed indicators and stall warning indicators (e.g., airplane buffet, stall horn, etc.).
AI.X.B.R6	Unacknowledged stall warning indications.

AI.X.B.R7	Effects of environmental elements on airplane performance and controllability. (e.g., turbulence, microbursts, and high density altitude).
AI.X.B.R8	Collision hazards.
AI.X.B.R9	Maneuvering at critically slow airspeeds.

Skills:	The applicant demonstrates and simultaneously explains how to:
AI.X.B.S1	Conduct and explain the procedure, manage the associated risk, and fly the airplane, while maintaining altitude ±100 feet, airspeed +5/-0 knots, heading ±10°, and specified bank angle ±5°, as appropriate.
AI.X.B.S2	Select an altitude that allows the maneuver to be performed no lower than 1,500 feet above ground level (AGL).
AI.X.B.S3	Clear the area.
AI.X.B.S4	Clean configuration demonstration:
AI.X.B.S4a	a. Establish and maintain design/operating maneuvering speed appropriate to the airplane's weight while describing pitch, power, and trim inputs to maintain altitude and airspeed, then;
AI.X.B.S4b	b. With gear and flaps retracted (as applicable), slow the airplane to, and maintain, best glide speed (or as specified by evaluator), noting the power setting required, then;
AI.X.B.S4c	c. Continue to slow the airplane to, and maintain, an airspeed at which any further increase in angle of attack, increase in load factor, or reduction in power would result in an immediate stall, and maintain that airspeed in level flight, noting the airspeed and power setting required, while;
AI.X.B.S4d	d. Verbally acknowledging stall warning indications, then;
AI.X.B.S4e	e. Without changing power setting, lower the pitch attitude and accelerate to a faster airspeed until reestablishing the airplane in level flight, noting the new airspeed and amount of altitude lost, then;
AI.X.B.S4f	f. Return to normal cruise flight at the altitude and heading specified by the evaluator
AI.X.B.S5	Landing configuration demonstration.
AI.X.B.S5a	a. Establish and maintain design/operating maneuvering speed appropriate to the airplane's weight while describing pitch, power, and trim inputs to maintain altitude and airspeed, then;
AI.X.B.S5b	b. Slow the airplane to, and maintain, the appropriate limiting airspeeds and fully extend the landing gear and flaps (as appropriate), then;
AI.X.B.S5c	c. With gear and flaps fully extended (as applicable), slow the airplane to, and maintain, reference landing speed (or as specified by the evaluator), noting the power setting required, then;
AI.X.B.S5d	d. With gear and flaps fully extended, continue to slow the airplane to, and maintain, an airspeed at which any further increase in angle of attack, increase in load factor, or reduction in power would result in an immediate stall, and maintain that airspeed in level flight, noting the airspeed and power setting required, while;
AI.X.B.S5e	e. Verbally acknowledging stall warning indications, then;
AI.X.B.S5f	f. Without changing power setting, lower the pitch attitude and accelerate to a faster airspeed until reestablishing the airplane in in level flight, noting the new airspeed and amount of altitude lost, then;
AI.X.B.S5g	g. Return to normal cruise flight at the altitude and heading specified by the evaluator
AI.X.B.S6	Analyze and correct common errors related to this Task.

Task C. Power-Off Stalls

References: *AC 61-67; FAA-H-8083-2, FAA-H-8083-3, FAA-H-8083-9, FAA-H-8083-25; POH/AFM*

Objective: To determine the applicant understands power-off stalls, can apply that knowledge, manage associated risks, demonstrate appropriate skills, and provide effective instruction.

Note: *See Appendix 2: Safety of Flight and Appendix 3: Aircraft, Equipment, and Operational Requirements & Limitations for information related to this Task.*

Knowledge:	The applicant demonstrates instructional knowledge by describing and explaining:
AI.X.C.K1	Purpose of and procedures for power-off stalls.
AI.X.C.K2	Aerodynamics associated with stalls in various airplane configurations, including the relationship between angle of attack, airspeed, load factor, power setting, airplane weight and center of gravity, airplane attitude, and yaw effects.
AI.X.C.K3	Stall characteristics as they relate to airplane design, and recognition impending stall and full stall indications using sight, sound, or feel.
AI.X.C.K4	Factors and situations that can lead to a power-off stall and actions that can be taken to prevent it.
AI.X.C.K5	Fundamentals of stall recovery.
AI.X.C.K6	Common errors related to this Task.

Risk Management:	The applicant explains and teaches how to identify and manage risk associated with:
AI.X.C.R1	Factors and situations that could lead to an inadvertent power-off stall, spin, and loss of control.
AI.X.C.R2	Range and limitations of stall warning indicators (e.g., aircraft buffet, stall horn, etc.).
AI.X.C.R3	Stall warning(s) during normal operations.
AI.X.C.R4	Stall recovery procedure.
AI.X.C.R5	Secondary stalls, accelerated stalls, and cross-control stalls.
AI.X.C.R6	Effect of environmental elements on airplane performance related to power-off stalls (e.g., turbulence, microbursts, and high-density altitude).
AI.X.C.R7	Collision hazards.
AI.X.C.R8	Distractions, task prioritization, loss of situational awareness, or disorientation.

Skills:	The applicant demonstrates and simultaneously explains how to:
AI.X.C.S1	Clear the area.
AI.X.C.S2	Select an entry altitude that allows the Task to be completed no lower than 1,500 feet above ground level (AGL) (ASEL, ASES) or 3,000 feet AGL (AMEL, AMES).
AI.X.C.S3	Configure the airplane in the approach or landing configuration, as specified by the evaluator, and maintain coordinated flight throughout the maneuver.
AI.X.C.S4	Establish a stabilized descent.
AI.X.C.S5	Transition smoothly from the approach or landing attitude to a pitch attitude that induces a stall.
AI.X.C.S6	Maintain a specified heading, ±10° if in straight flight; maintain a specified angle of bank not to exceed 20°, ±5° if in turning flight, until an impending or full stall occurs, as specified by the evaluator.
AI.X.C.S7	Acknowledge the cues at the first indication of a stall (e.g., aircraft buffet, stall horn, etc.).
AI.X.C.S8	Recover at the first indication of a stall or after a full stall has occurred, as specified by the evaluator.

Flight Instructor – Airplane ACS (FAA-S-ACS-25)

AI.X.C.S9	Configure the airplane as recommended by the manufacturer, and accelerate to best angle of climb speed (V_X) or best rate of climb speed (V_Y).
AI.X.C.S10	Return to the altitude, heading, and airspeed specified by the evaluator.
AI.X.C.S11	Analyze and correct common errors related to this Task.

Task D. Power-On Stalls

References: AC 61-67; FAA-H-8083-2, FAA-H-8083-3, FAA-H-8083-9, FAA-H-8083-25; POH/AFM

Objective: To determine the applicant understands power-on stalls, can apply that knowledge, manage associated risks, demonstrate appropriate skills, and provide effective instruction.

Note: See Appendix 2: Safety of Flight and Appendix 3: Aircraft, Equipment, and Operational Requirements & Limitations for information related to this Task.

Knowledge:	The applicant demonstrates instructional knowledge by describing and explaining:
AI.X.D.K1	Purpose of and procedures for power-on stalls.
AI.X.D.K2	Aerodynamics associated with stalls in various airplane configurations, including the relationship between angle of attack, airspeed, load factor, power setting, airplane weight and center of gravity, airplane attitude, and yaw effects.
AI.X.D.K3	Stall characteristics as they relate to airplane design, and recognition impending stall and full stall indications using sight, sound, or feel.
AI.X.D.K4	Factors and situations that can lead to a power-on stall and actions that can be taken to prevent it.
AI.X.D.K5	Fundamentals of stall recovery.
AI.X.D.K6	Common errors related to this Task.

Risk Management:	The applicant explains and teaches how to identify and manage risk associated with:
AI.X.D.R1	Factors and situations that could lead to an inadvertent power-on stall, spin, and loss of control.
AI.X.D.R2	Range and limitations of stall warning indicators (e.g., aircraft buffet, stall horn, etc.).
AI.X.D.R3	Stall warning(s) during normal operations.
AI.X.D.R4	Stall recovery procedure.
AI.X.D.R5	Secondary stalls, accelerated stalls, elevator trim stalls, and cross-control stalls.
AI.X.D.R6	Effect of environmental elements on airplane performance related to power-on stalls (e.g., turbulence, microbursts, and high-density altitude).
AI.X.D.R7	Collision hazards.
AI.X.D.R8	Distractions, task prioritization, loss of situational awareness, or disorientation.

Skills:	The applicant demonstrates and simultaneously explains how to:
AI.X.D.S1	Clear the area.
AI.X.D.S2	Select an entry altitude that allows the Task to be completed no lower than 1,500 feet above ground level (AGL) (ASEL, ASES) or 3,000 feet AGL (AMEL, AMES).
AI.X.D.S3	Establish the takeoff, departure, or cruise configuration, as specified by the evaluator, and maintain coordinated flight throughout the maneuver.
AI.X.D.S4	Set power to no less than 65 percent power.

Al.X.D.S5	Transition smoothly from the takeoff or departure attitude to the pitch attitude that induces a stall.
Al.X.D.S6	Maintain a specified heading ±10° if in straight flight; maintain a specified angle of bank not to exceed 20°, ±10° if in turning flight, until an impending or full stall is reached, as specified by the evaluator.
Al.X.D.S7	Acknowledge the cues at the first indication of a stall (e.g., aircraft buffet, stall horn, etc.).
Al.X.D.S8	Recover at the first indication of a stall or after a full stall has occurred, as specified by the evaluator.
Al.X.D.S9	Configure the airplane as recommended by the manufacturer, and accelerate to best angle of climb speed (V_X) or best rate of climb speed (V_Y).
Al.X.D.S10	Return to the altitude, heading, and airspeed specified by the evaluator.
Al.X.D.S11	Analyze and correct common errors related to this Task.

Task E. Accelerated Stalls

References: AC 61-67; FAA-H-8083-2, FAA-H-8083-3, FAA-H-8083-9, FAA-H-8083-25; POH/AFM

Objective: To determine the applicant understands accelerated stalls (power-on and power-off), can apply that knowledge, manage associated risks, demonstrate appropriate skills, and provide effective instruction.

Note: See Appendix 2: Safety of Flight and Appendix 3: Aircraft, Equipment, and Operational Requirements & Limitations for information related to this Task.

Knowledge:	The applicant demonstrates instructional knowledge by describing and explaining:
Al.X.E.K1	Purpose of and procedures for accelerated stalls.
Al.X.E.K2	Aerodynamics associated with accelerated stalls in various airplane configurations, including the relationship between angle of attack, airspeed, load factor, power setting, airplane weight and center of gravity, airplane attitude, and yaw effects.
Al.X.E.K3	Stall characteristics as they relate to airplane design, and recognition impending stall and full stall indications using sight, sound, or feel.
Al.X.E.K4	Factors leading to an accelerated stall and preventive actions.
Al.X.E.K5	Fundamentals of stall recovery.
Al.X.E.K6	Common errors related to this Task.

Risk Management:	The applicant explains and teaches how to identify and manage risk associated with:
Al.X.E.R1	Factors and situations that could lead to an inadvertent accelerated stall, spin, and loss of control.
Al.X.E.R2	Range and limitations of stall warning indicators (e.g., aircraft buffet, stall horn, etc.).
Al.X.E.R3	Stall warning(s) during normal operations.
Al.X.E.R4	Stall recovery procedure.
Al.X.E.R5	Secondary stalls, cross-control stalls, and spins.
Al.X.E.R6	Effect of environmental elements on airplane performance related to accelerated stalls (e.g., turbulence, microbursts, and high-density altitude).

Flight Instructor – Airplane ACS (FAA-S-ACS-25)

AI.X.E.R7	Collision hazards.
AI.X.E.R8	Distractions, task prioritization, loss of situational awareness, or disorientation.

Skills:	The applicant demonstrates and simultaneously explains how to:
AI.X.E.S1	Clear the area.
AI.X.E.S2	Select an entry altitude that allows the Task to be completed no lower than 3,000 feet above ground level (AGL).
AI.X.E.S3	Establish the configuration as specified by the evaluator.
AI.X.E.S4	Set power appropriate for the configuration, such that the airspeed does not exceed the maneuvering speed (V_A) or any other applicable Pilot's Operating Handbook (POH)/Airplane Flight Manual (AFM) limitation.
AI.X.E.S5	Establish and maintain a coordinated turn in a 45° bank, increasing elevator back pressure smoothly and firmly until an impending stall is reached.
AI.X.E.S6	Acknowledge the cues at the first indication of a stall (e.g., aircraft buffet, stall horn, etc.).
AI.X.E.S7	Execute a stall recovery in accordance with procedures set forth in the Pilot's Operating Handbook (POH)/Flight Manual (FM).
AI.X.E.S8	Configure the airplane as recommended by the manufacturer, and accelerate to best angle of climb speed (V_X) or best rate of climb speed (V_Y).
AI.X.E.S9	Return to the altitude, heading, and airspeed specified by the evaluator.
AI.X.E.S10	Analyze and correct common errors related to this Task.

Task F. Cross-Controlled Stall Demonstration (ASEL, ASES)

References: AC 61-67; FAA-H-8083-2, FAA-H-8083-3, FAA-H-8083-9, FAA-H-8083-25; POH/AFM

Objective: To determine the applicant understands cross-controlled stalls, can apply that knowledge, manage associated risks, demonstrate appropriate skills, and provide effective instruction.

Note: See Appendix 2: Safety of Flight and Appendix 3: Aircraft, Equipment, and Operational Requirements & Limitations for information related to this Task.

Knowledge:	The applicant demonstrates instructional knowledge by describing and explaining:
AI.X.F.K1	Aerodynamics of cross-controlled stalls.
AI.X.F.K2	Flight situations where unintentional cross-controlled stalls may occur.
AI.X.F.K3	Recognition of cross-controlled stalls.
AI.X.F.K4	Entry procedure and minimum entry altitude.
AI.X.F.K5	Recovery procedure.
AI.X.F.K6	Common errors related to this Task.

Risk Management:	The applicant explains and teaches how to identify and manage risk associated with:
AI.X.F.R1	Stall recovery procedure.
AI.X.F.R2	Effect of environmental elements on airplane performance related to cross-controlled stalls (e.g., turbulence, microbursts, and high-density altitude).
AI.X.F.R3	Collision hazards.

AI.X.F.R4	Aircraft limitations.
AI.X.F.R5	Distractions, task prioritization, loss of situational awareness, or disorientation.

Skills:	The applicant exhibits the skill to:
AI.X.F.S1	Clear the area.
AI.X.F.S2	Select an entry altitude that allows the Task to be completed no lower than 3,000 feet above ground level (AGL).
AI.X.F.S3	Configure the airplane (with gear down) and close the throttle.
AI.X.F.S4	Establish a normal glide airspeed and trim the airplane.
AI.X.F.S5	Roll into a medium-banked turn, apply excess rudder in the turn while holding bank constant with opposite aileron input, and add elevator pressure to keep the nose from lowering.
AI.X.F.S6	Acknowledge the cues at the first indication of a stall (e.g., aircraft buffet, stall horn, etc.).
AI.X.F.S7	Recover at the first indication of a stall or after a full stall has occurred, as specified by the evaluator.
AI.X.F.S8	Describe and demonstrate conditions that lead to a cross-controlled stall for future avoidance.
AI.X.F.S9	Analyze and correct common errors related to this Task.

Task G. Elevator Trim Stall Demonstration (ASEL, ASES)

References: AC 61-67; FAA-H-8083-2, FAA-H-8083-3, FAA-H-8083-9, FAA-H-8083-25; POH/AFM

Objective: To determine the applicant understands elevator trim stalls, can apply that knowledge, manage associated risks, demonstrate appropriate skills, and provide effective instruction.

Note: See Appendix 2: Safety of Flight and Appendix 3: Aircraft, Equipment, and Operational Requirements & Limitations for information related to this Task.

Knowledge:	The applicant demonstrates instructional knowledge by describing and explaining:
AI.X.G.K1	Aerodynamics of elevator trim stalls.
AI.X.G.K2	Flight situations where elevator trim stalls could occur.
AI.X.G.K3	Recognition of elevator trim stalls.
AI.X.G.K4	Entry procedure and minimum entry altitude.
AI.X.G.K5	Recovery procedure.
AI.X.G.K6	Common errors related to this Task.

Risk Management:	The applicant explains and teaches how to identify and manage risk associated with:
AI.X.G.R1	Stall recovery procedure.
AI.X.G.R2	Effect of environmental elements on airplane performance related to cross-controlled stalls (e.g., turbulence, microbursts, and high-density altitude).
AI.X.G.R3	Collision hazards.
AI.X.G.R4	Aircraft limitations.
AI.X.G.R5	Distractions, task prioritization, loss of situational awareness, or disorientation.

Skills:	The applicant exhibits the skill to:

AI.X.G.S1	Clear the area.
AI.X.G.S2	Select an entry altitude that allows the Task to be completed no lower than 3,000 feet above ground level (AGL).
AI.X.G.S3	Retard the throttle and configure the airplane for landing.
AI.X.G.S4	Establish a normal glide airspeed and trim the airplane.
AI.X.G.S5	Advance the throttle to the maximum allowable power as in a go-around.
AI.X.G.S6	Acknowledge the cues at the first indication of a stall (e.g., aircraft buffet, stall horn, etc.).
AI.X.G.S7	Recover at the first indication of a stall or after a full stall has occurred, as specified by the evaluator.
AI.X.G.S8	Adjust trim and return to the desired flightpath.
AI.X.G.S9	Describe and demonstrate conditions that lead to an elevator trim stall for future avoidance.
AI.X.G.S10	Analyze and correct common errors related to this Task.

Task H. Secondary Stall Demonstration (ASEL, ASES)

References: AC 61-67; FAA-H-8083-2, FAA-H-8083-3, FAA-H-8083-9, FAA-H-8083-25; POH/AFM

Objective: To determine the applicant understands secondary stalls, can apply that knowledge, manage associated risks, demonstrate appropriate skills, and provide effective instruction.

Note: See Appendix 2: Safety of Flight and Appendix 3: Aircraft, Equipment, and Operational Requirements & Limitations for information related to this Task.

Knowledge:	The applicant demonstrates instructional knowledge by describing and explaining:
AI.X.H.K1	Aerodynamics of secondary stalls.
AI.X.H.K2	Flight situations where secondary stalls may occur.
AI.X.H.K3	Recognition of a secondary stall.
AI.X.H.K4	Entry procedure and minimum entry altitude.
AI.X.H.K5	Recovery procedure.
AI.X.H.K6	Common errors related to this Task.

Risk Management:	The applicant explains and teaches how to identify and manage risk associated with:
AI.X.H.R1	Stall recovery procedure.
AI.X.H.R2	Effect of environmental elements on airplane performance related to cross-controlled stalls (e.g., turbulence, microbursts, and high-density altitude).
AI.X.H.R3	Collision hazards.
AI.X.H.R4	Aircraft limitations.
AI.X.H.R5	Distractions, task prioritization, loss of situational awareness, or disorientation.

Skills:	The applicant exhibits the skill to:
AI.X.H.S1	Clear the area.

AI.X.H.S2	Select an entry altitude that allows the Task to be completed no lower than 3,000 feet above ground level (AGL).
AI.X.H.S3	Enter a stall in a specified configuration and exceed the critical angle of attach a second time during the recovery.
AI.X.H.S4	Recover promptly and appropriately after a secondary stall occurs.
AI.X.H.S5	Describe and demonstrate conditions that lead to a secondary stall for future avoidance.
AI.X.H.S6	Analyze and correct common errors related to this Task.

Task I. Spin Awareness and Spins

References: AC 61-67; FAA-H-8083-2, FAA-H-8083-3, FAA-H-8083-9, FAA-H-8083-25; POH/AFM

Objective: To determine the applicant understands spins, can apply that knowledge, manage associated risks, demonstrate appropriate skills, and provide effective instruction.

Note: At the discretion of the evaluator, a logbook record attesting applicant instructional competency in spin entries, spins, and spin recoveries may be accepted in lieu of this Task. The flight instructor who conducted the spin instruction must certify the logbook record.

Note: See Appendix 2: Safety of Flight and Appendix 3: Aircraft, Equipment, and Operational Requirements & Limitations for information related to this Task.

Knowledge:	The applicant demonstrates instructional knowledge by describing and explaining:
AI.X.I.K1	Purpose of and procedures for spin awareness and spins.
AI.X.I.K2	Aerodynamics associated with spins in various airplane configurations, including the relationship between angle of attack, airspeed, load factor, power setting, airplane weight and center of gravity, airplane attitude, and yaw effects.
AI.X.I.K3	What causes a spin and how to identify the entry, incipient, and developed phases of a spin.
AI.X.I.K4	Spin recovery procedure.
AI.X.I.K5	Human factors associated with spin instruction.
AI.X.I.K6	How to determine if an airplane approved for the spin maneuver based on airworthiness category and type certificate.
AI.X.I.K7	Flight situations where unintentional spins may occur.
AI.X.I.K8	Entry procedure and minimum entry altitude for intentional spins.
AI.X.I.K9	Control procedure to maintain a stabilized spin.
AI.X.I.K10	Recognize conditions that lead to a spin for future avoidance.
AI.X.I.K11	Orientation during a spin, including which instrument(s) are reliable for determining the directions of spin.
AI.X.I.K12	Recovery procedure and minimum recovery altitude for intentional spins.
AI.X.I.K13	Common errors related to this Task.

Risk Management:	The applicant explains and teaches how to identify and manage risk associated with:
AI.X.I.R1	Factors and situations that could lead to inadvertent spin and loss of control.
AI.X.I.R2	Range and limitations of stall warning indicators (e.g., aircraft buffet, stall horn, etc.).

AI.X.I.R3	Spin recovery procedure.
AI.X.I.R4	Effect of environmental elements on airplane performance related to spins (e.g., turbulence, microbursts, and high-density altitude).
AI.X.I.R5	Collision hazards.
AI.X.I.R6	Distractions, task prioritization, loss of situational awareness, or disorientation.

Skills:	The applicant demonstrates and simultaneously explains how to:
AI.X.I.S1	Clear the area.
AI.X.I.S2	Select an entry altitude that allows the Task to be completed no lower than 4,000 feet AGL.
AI.X.I.S3	Enter and recover from an intentional spin if requested by the evaluator.
AI.X.I.S4	Analyze and correct common errors related to this Task.

Area of Operation XI. Basic Instrument Maneuvers

Note: *The evaluator must select at least one Task from this Area of Operation.*

Task A. Straight-and-Level Flight

References: *FAA-H-8083-2, FAA-H-8083-3, FAA-H-8083-9, FAA-H-8083-15, FAA-H-8083-16, FAA-H-8083-25; POH/AFM*

Objective: To determine the applicant understands attitude instrument flying during straight-and-level flight, can apply that knowledge, manage associated risks, demonstrate appropriate skills, and provide effective instruction, solely by reference to instruments.

Knowledge:	The applicant demonstrates instructional knowledge by describing and explaining:
AI.XI.A.K1	Flight instruments as they relate to:
AI.XI.A.K1a	a. Instrument limitations and potential errors
AI.XI.A.K1b	b. Indication of the aircraft attitude
AI.XI.A.K1c	c. Function and operation
AI.XI.A.K1d	d. Proper instrument cross-check techniques
AI.XI.A.K2	Common errors related to this Task.

Risk Management:	The applicant explains and teaches how to identify and manage risk associated with:
AI.XI.A.R1	Instrument flying hazards, including failure to maintain visual flight rules (VFR), spatial disorientation, loss of control, fatigue, stress, and emergency off airport landings.
AI.XI.A.R2	When to seek assistance or declare an emergency in a deteriorating situation.
AI.XI.A.R3	Collision hazards.
AI.XI.A.R4	Distractions, task prioritization, loss of situational awareness, or disorientation.
AI.XI.A.R5	Fixation and omission.
AI.XI.A.R6	Instrument Interpretation.
AI.XI.A.R7	Control application solely by reference to instruments.
AI.XI.A.R8	Trimming the aircraft.

Skills:	The applicant demonstrates and simultaneously explains how to:
AI.XI.A.S1	Maintain straight-and-level flight using proper instrument cross-check and interpretation, and coordinated control application.
AI.XI.A.S2	Maintain altitude ±100 feet, heading ±10°, and airspeed ±10 knots.
AI.XI.A.S3	Analyze and correct common errors related to this Task.

Task B. Constant Airspeed Climbs

References: *FAA-H-8083-2, FAA-H-8083-3, FAA-H-8083-9, FAA-H-8083-15, FAA-H-8083-16, FAA-H-8083-25; POH/AFM*

Objective: To determine the applicant understands attitude instrument flying during constant airspeed climbs, can apply that knowledge, manage associated risks, demonstrate appropriate skills, and provide effective instruction, solely by reference to instruments.

Knowledge:	The applicant demonstrates instructional knowledge by describing and explaining:
AI.XI.B.K1	Flight instruments as they relate to:
AI.XI.B.K1a	a. Instrument limitations and potential errors
AI.XI.B.K1b	b. Indication of the aircraft attitude
AI.XI.B.K1c	c. Function and operation
AI.XI.B.K1d	d. Proper instrument cross-check techniques
AI.XI.B.K2	Common errors related to this Task.

Risk Management:	The applicant explains and teaches how to identify and manage risk associated with:
AI.XI.B.R1	Instrument flying hazards, including failure to maintain visual flight rules (VFR), spatial disorientation, loss of control, fatigue, stress, and emergency off airport landings.
AI.XI.B.R2	When to seek assistance or declare an emergency in a deteriorating situation.
AI.XI.B.R3	Collision hazards.
AI.XI.B.R4	Distractions, task prioritization, loss of situational awareness, or disorientation.
AI.XI.B.R5	Fixation and omission.
AI.XI.B.R6	Instrument Interpretation.
AI.XI.B.R7	Control application solely by reference to instruments.
AI.XI.B.R8	Trimming the aircraft.

Skills:	The applicant demonstrates and simultaneously explains how to:
AI.XI.B.S1	Transition to the climb pitch attitude and power setting on an assigned heading using proper instrument cross-check and interpretation, and coordinated flight control application.
AI.XI.B.S2	Climb at a constant airspeed to specific altitudes in straight flight and turns.
AI.XI.B.S3	Level off at the assigned altitude and maintain altitude ±100 feet, heading ±10°, and airspeed ±10 knots.
AI.XI.B.S4	Analyze and correct common errors related to this Task.

Task C. Constant Airspeed Descents

References: *FAA-H-8083-2, FAA-H-8083-3, FAA-H-8083-9, FAA-H-8083-15, FAA-H-8083-16, FAA-H-8083-25; POH/AFM*

Objective: To determine the applicant understands attitude instrument flying during constant airspeed descents, can apply that knowledge, manage associated risks, demonstrate appropriate skills, and provide effective instruction, solely by reference to instruments.

Knowledge: The applicant demonstrates instructional knowledge by describing and explaining:

AI.XI.C.K1	Flight instruments as they relate to:
AI.XI.C.K1a	a. Instrument limitations and potential errors
AI.XI.C.K1b	b. Indication of the aircraft attitude
AI.XI.C.K1c	c. Function and operation
AI.XI.C.K1d	d. Proper instrument cross-check techniques
AI.XI.C.K2	Common errors related to this Task.

Risk Management: The applicant explains and teaches how to identify and manage risk associated with:

AI.XI.C.R1	Instrument flying hazards, including failure to maintain visual flight rules (VFR), spatial disorientation, loss of control, fatigue, stress, and emergency off airport landings.
AI.XI.C.R2	When to seek assistance or declare an emergency in a deteriorating situation.
AI.XI.C.R3	Collision hazards.
AI.XI.C.R4	Distractions, task prioritization, loss of situational awareness, or disorientation.
AI.XI.C.R5	Fixation and omission.
AI.XI.C.R6	Instrument Interpretation.
AI.XI.C.R7	Control application solely by reference to instruments.
AI.XI.C.R8	Trimming the aircraft.

Skills: The applicant demonstrates and simultaneously explains how to:

AI.XI.C.S1	Transition to the descent pitch attitude and power setting on an assigned heading using proper instrument cross-check and interpretation, and coordinated flight control application.
AI.XI.C.S2	Descend at a constant airspeed to specific altitudes in straight flight and turns.
AI.XI.C.S3	Level off at the assigned altitude and maintain altitude ±100 feet, heading ±10°, and airspeed ±10 knots.
AI.XI.C.S4	Analyze and correct common errors related to this Task.

Task D. Turns to Headings

References: FAA-H-8083-2, FAA-H-8083-3, FAA-H-8083-9, FAA-H-8083-15, FAA-H-8083-16, FAA-H-8083-25; POH/AFM

Objective: To determine the applicant understands attitude instrument flying during turns to headings, can apply that knowledge, manage associated risks, demonstrate appropriate skills, and provide effective instruction, solely by reference to instruments.

Knowledge: The applicant demonstrates instructional knowledge by describing and explaining:

AI.XI.D.K1	Flight instruments as they relate to:
AI.XI.D.K1a	a. Instrument limitations and potential errors
AI.XI.D.K1b	b. Indication of the aircraft attitude
AI.XI.D.K1c	c. Function and operation
AI.XI.D.K1d	d. Proper instrument cross-check techniques

Al.XI.D.K2	Common errors related to this Task.

Risk Management: The applicant explains and teaches how to identify and manage risk associated with:

Al.XI.D.R1	Instrument flying hazards, including failure to maintain visual flight rules (VFR), spatial disorientation, loss of control, fatigue, stress, and emergency off airport landings.
Al.XI.D.R2	When to seek assistance or declare an emergency in a deteriorating situation.
Al.XI.D.R3	Collision hazards.
Al.XI.D.R4	Distractions, task prioritization, loss of situational awareness, or disorientation.
Al.XI.D.R5	Fixation and omission.
Al.XI.D.R6	Instrument Interpretation.
Al.XI.D.R7	Control application solely by reference to instruments.
Al.XI.D.R8	Trimming the aircraft.

Skills: The applicant demonstrates and simultaneously explains how to:

Al.XI.D.S1	Turns to headings, maintain altitude ±100 feet, maintain a standard rate turn, roll out on the assigned heading ±10°, and maintain airspeed ±10 knots.
Al.XI.D.S2	Analyze and correct common errors related to this Task.

Task E. Recovery from Unusual Flight Attitudes

References: FAA-H-8083-2, FAA-H-8083-3, FAA-H-8083-9, FAA-H-8083-15, FAA-H-8083-16, FAA-H-8083-25; POH/AFM

Objective: To determine the applicant understands attitude instrument flying while recovering from unusual attitudes, can apply that knowledge, manage associated risks, demonstrate appropriate skills, and provide effective instruction, solely by reference to instruments.

Knowledge: The applicant demonstrates instructional knowledge by describing and explaining:

Al.XI.E.K1	Prevention of unusual attitudes, including flight causal, physiological, and environmental factors, and system and equipment failures.
Al.XI.E.K2	Procedures for recovery from unusual attitudes in flight.
Al.XI.E.K3	Procedures available to safely regain visual meteorological conditions (VMC) after flight into inadvertent instrument meteorological conditions or unintended instrument meteorological conditions (IIMC)/(UIMC).
Al.XI.E.K4	Appropriate use of automation, if applicable.
Al.XI.E.K5	Common errors related to this Task.

Risk Management: The applicant explains and teaches how to identify and manage risk associated with:

Al.XI.E.R1	Situations that could lead to loss of control in-flight (LOC-I) or unusual attitudes in-flight (e.g., stress, task saturation, inadequate instrument scan distractions, and spatial disorientation).
Al.XI.E.R2	Assessment of the unusual attitude.
Al.XI.E.R3	Control input errors, inducing undesired aircraft attitudes.
Al.XI.E.R4	Collision hazards.

AI.XI.E.R5	Distractions, task prioritization, loss of situational awareness, or disorientation.
AI.XI.E.R6	Interpreting flight instruments.
AI.XI.E.R7	Control application solely by reference to instruments.
AI.XI.E.R8	Operating envelope considerations.

Skills:	The applicant demonstrates and simultaneously explains how to:
AI.XI.E.S1	Use proper instrument cross-check and interpretation to identify an unusual attitude (including both nose-high and nose-low) in flight, and apply the appropriate flight control, power input, and aircraft configuration in the correct sequence, to return to a stabilized level flight attitude.
AI.XI.E.S2	Use single-pilot resource management (SRM) or crew resource management (CRM), as appropriate.
AI.XI.E.S3	Analyze and correct common errors related to this Task.

Area of Operation XII. Emergency Operations

Note: *For ASEL or ASES, the evaluator must select at least Tasks B and C. For AMEL or AMES, the evaluator must select Tasks E or F; Task G; and at least one other Task.*

Task A. Emergency Descent

References: *FAA-H-8083-2, FAA-H-8083-3, FAA-H-8083-9, FAA-H-8083-23, FAA-H-8083-25; POH/AFM*

Objective: To determine the applicant understands emergency descent, can apply that knowledge, manage associated risks, demonstrate appropriate skills, and provide effective instruction.

Note: *See Appendix 2: Safety of Flight.*

Knowledge:	The applicant demonstrates instructional knowledge by describing and explaining:
AI.XII.A.K1	Purpose of and procedures for emergency descent.
AI.XII.A.K2	Situations that would require an emergency descent (e.g., depressurization, smoke, or engine fire).
AI.XII.A.K3	Immediate action items and emergency procedures.
AI.XII.A.K4	Aircraft performance and limitations.
AI.XII.A.K5	Airspeed, including airspeed limitations.
AI.XII.A.K6	Common errors related to this Task.

Risk Management:	The applicant explains and teaches how to identify and manage risk associated with:
AI.XII.A.R1	Altitude, wind, terrain, obstructions, gliding distance, and available landing distance considerations.
AI.XII.A.R2	Collision hazards.
AI.XII.A.R3	Configuring the airplane.
AI.XII.A.R4	Distractions, task prioritization, loss of situational awareness, or disorientation.

Skills:	The applicant demonstrates and simultaneously explains how to:
AI.XII.A.S1	Clear the area.
AI.XII.A.S2	Establish and maintain the appropriate airspeed and configuration appropriate to the scenario specified by the evaluator and as covered in Pilot's Operating Handbook (POH)/Airplane Flight Manual (AFM) for the emergency descent.
AI.XII.A.S3	Maintain orientation, divide attention appropriately, and plan and execute a smooth recovery.
AI.XII.A.S4	Use bank angle between 30° and 45° to maintain positive load factors during the descent.
AI.XII.A.S5	Maintain appropriate airspeed +0/-10 knots, and level off at a specified altitude ±100 feet.
AI.XII.A.S6	Complete the appropriate checklist(s).
AI.XII.A.S7	Analyze and correct common errors related to this Task.

Task B. Emergency Approach and Landing (Simulated) (ASEL, ASES)

References: *FAA-H-8083-2, FAA-H-8083-3, FAA-H-8083-9, FAA-H-8083-23, FAA-H-8083-25; POH/AFM*

Objective: To determine the applicant understands power failure at altitude and associated emergency approach and landing procedures, can apply that knowledge, manage associated risks, demonstrate appropriate skills, and provide effective instruction.

Note: *See Appendix 2: Safety of Flight and Appendix 3: Aircraft, Equipment, and Operational Requirements & Limitations for information related to this Task.*

Knowledge:	The applicant demonstrates instructional knowledge by describing and explaining:
AI.XII.B.K1	Immediate action items and emergency procedures.
AI.XII.B.K2	Airspeed, including:
AI.XII.B.K2a	a. Importance of best glide speed and its relationship to distance
AI.XII.B.K2b	b. Difference between best glide speed and minimum sink speed
AI.XII.B.K2c	c. Effects of wind on glide distance
AI.XII.B.K3	Effects of atmospheric conditions on emergency approach and landing.
AI.XII.B.K4	A stabilized approach, including energy management concepts.
AI.XII.B.K5	Emergency Locator Transmitters (ELTs) and other emergency locating devices.
AI.XII.B.K6	Air traffic control (ATC) services to aircraft in distress.
AI.XII.B.K7	Common errors related to this Task.

Risk Management:	The applicant explains and teaches how to identify and manage risk associated with:
AI.XII.B.R1	Altitude, wind, terrain, obstructions, gliding distance, and available landing distance considerations.
AI.XII.B.R2	Following or changing the planned flightpath to the selected landing area.
AI.XII.B.R3	Collision hazards.
AI.XII.B.R4	Configuring the airplane.
AI.XII.B.R5	Low altitude maneuvering, including stall, spin, or controlled flight into terrain (CFIT).
AI.XII.B.R6	Distractions, task prioritization, loss of situational awareness, or disorientation.

Skills:	The applicant demonstrates and simultaneously explains how to:
AI.XII.B.S1	Establish and maintain the recommended best glide airspeed, ±10 knots.
AI.XII.B.S2	Configure the airplane in accordance with the Pilot's Operating Handbook (POH)/Airplane Flight Manual (AFM) and existing conditions.
AI.XII.B.S3	Select a suitable landing area considering altitude, wind, terrain, obstructions, and available glide distance.
AI.XII.B.S4	Plan and follow a flightpath to the selected landing area considering altitude, wind, terrain, and obstructions.
AI.XII.B.S5	Prepare for landing as specified by the evaluator.
AI.XII.B.S6	Complete the appropriate checklist(s).
AI.XII.B.S7	Analyze and correct common errors related to this Task.

Task C. Systems and Equipment Malfunctions

References: *FAA-H-8083-2, FAA-H-8083-3, FAA-H-8083-9, FAA-H-8083-23, FAA-H-8083-25; POH/AFM*

Objective: To determine the applicant understands system and equipment malfunctions appropriate to the aircraft provided for the practical test, can apply that knowledge, manage associated risks, demonstrate appropriate skills, and provide effective instruction.

Knowledge:	The applicant demonstrates instructional knowledge by describing and explaining:
AI.XII.C.K1	Causes of partial or complete power loss related to the specific type of powerplant(s).
AI.XII.C.K2	System and equipment malfunctions specific to the aircraft, including:
AI.XII.C.K2a	a. Electrical malfunction
AI.XII.C.K2b	b. Vacuum/pressure and associated flight instrument malfunctions
AI.XII.C.K2c	c. Pitot-static system malfunction
AI.XII.C.K2d	d. Electronic flight deck display malfunction
AI.XII.C.K2e	e. Landing gear or flap malfunction
AI.XII.C.K2f	f. Inoperative trim
AI.XII.C.K3	Causes and remedies for smoke or fire onboard the aircraft.
AI.XII.C.K4	Any other system specific to the aircraft (e.g., supplemental oxygen, deicing).
AI.XII.C.K5	Inadvertent door or window opening.
AI.XII.C.K6	Common errors related to this Task.

Risk Management:	The applicant explains and teaches how to identify and manage risk associated with:
AI.XII.C.R1	Startle response.
AI.XII.C.R2	Checklist usage for a system or equipment malfunction.
AI.XII.C.R3	Distractions, task prioritization, loss of situational awareness, or disorientation.
AI.XII.C.R4	Undesired aircraft state.

Skills:	The applicant demonstrates and simultaneously explains how to:
AI.XII.C.S1	Determine appropriate action for simulated emergencies specified by the evaluator, from at least three of the elements or sub-elements listed in K1 through K5.
AI.XII.C.S2	Complete the appropriate checklist(s).
AI.XII.C.S3	Analyze and correct common errors related to this Task.

Task D. Emergency Equipment and Survival Gear

References: *FAA-H-8083-2, FAA-H-8083-3, FAA-H-8083-9, FAA-H-8083-23, FAA-H-8083-25; POH/AFM*

Objective: To determine the applicant understands emergency equipment and survival gear, can apply that knowledge, manage associated risks, demonstrate appropriate skills, and provide effective instruction.

Note: *See Appendix 3: Aircraft, Equipment, and Operational Requirements & Limitations for information related to this Task.*

Knowledge:	The applicant demonstrates instructional knowledge by describing and explaining:
AI.XII.D.K1	Emergency Locator Transmitter (ELT) operations, limitations, and testing requirements.
AI.XII.D.K2	Fire extinguisher operations and limitations.
AI.XII.D.K3	Emergency equipment and survival gear needed for:
AI.XII.D.K3a	a. Climate extremes (hot/cold)
AI.XII.D.K3b	b. Mountainous terrain
AI.XII.D.K3c	c. Overwater operations
AI.XII.D.K4	When to deploy a ballistic parachute and associated passenger briefings, if equipped.
AI.XII.D.K5	When to activate an emergency auto-land system and brief passengers, if equipped.
AI.XII.D.K6	Common errors related to this Task.

Risk Management:	The applicant explains and teaches how to identify and manage risk associated with:
AI.XII.D.R1	Survival gear (water, clothing, shelter) for 48 to 72 hours.
AI.XII.D.R2	Use of a ballistic parachute system.
AI.XII.D.R3	Use of an emergency auto-land system, if installed.

Skills:	The applicant demonstrates and simultaneously explains how to:
AI.XII.D.S1	Identify appropriate equipment and personal gear.
AI.XII.D.S2	Brief passengers on proper use of on-board emergency equipment and survival gear.
AI.XII.D.S3	Simulate ballistic parachute deployment procedures, if equipped.
AI.XII.D.S4	Analyze and correct common errors related to this Task.

Task E. Engine Failure During Takeoff Before V_{MC} (Simulated) (AMEL, AMES)

References: FAA-H-8083-2, FAA-H-8083-3, FAA-H-8083-9, FAA-H-8083-25; FAA-P-8740-66; POH/AFM

Objective: To determine the applicant understands engine failure during takeoff, can apply that knowledge, manage associated risks, demonstrate appropriate skills, and provide effective instruction.

Note: See Appendix 2: Safety of Flight and Appendix 3: Aircraft, Equipment, and Operational Requirements & Limitations for information related to this Task.

Knowledge:	The applicant demonstrates instructional knowledge by describing and explaining:
AI.XII.E.K1	Factors affecting minimum controllable speed (V_{MC}).
AI.XII.E.K2	V_{MC} (red line) and best single-engine rate of climb airspeed (V_{YSE}) (blue line).
AI.XII.E.K3	Accelerate/stop distance.
AI.XII.E.K4	Common errors related to this Task.

Risk Management:	The applicant explains and teaches how to identify and manage risk associated with:
AI.XII.E.R1	Potential engine failure during takeoff.
AI.XII.E.R2	Configuring the airplane.
AI.XII.E.R3	Distractions, task prioritization, loss of situational awareness, or disorientation.

Skills:	The applicant demonstrates and simultaneously explains how to:
AI.XII.E.S1	Close the throttles smoothly and promptly when a simulated engine failure occurs.
AI.XII.E.S2	Maintain directional control and apply brakes (AMEL), or flight controls (AMES), as necessary.
AI.XII.E.S3	Analyze and correct common errors related to this Task.

Task F. Engine Failure After Liftoff (Simulated) (AMEL, AMES)

References: *FAA-H-8083-2, FAA-H-8083-3, FAA-H-8083-9, FAA-H-8083-25; FAA-P-8740-66; POH/AFM*

Objective: To determine the applicant understands engine failure after liftoff, can apply that knowledge, manage associated risks, demonstrate appropriate skills, and provide effective instruction.

Note: *See Appendix 2: Safety of Flight and Appendix 3: Aircraft, Equipment, and Operational Requirements & Limitations for information related to this Task.*

Knowledge:	The applicant demonstrates instructional knowledge by describing and explaining:
AI.XII.F.K1	Factors affecting minimum controllable speed (V_{MC}).
AI.XII.F.K2	V_{MC} (red line), V_{YSE} (blue line), and safe single-engine speed (V_{SSE}).
AI.XII.F.K3	Accelerate/stop and accelerate/go distances.
AI.XII.F.K4	How to identify, verify, feather, and secure an inoperative engine.
AI.XII.F.K5	Importance of drag reduction, including propeller feathering, gear and flap retraction, the manufacturer's recommended control input and its relation to zero sideslip.
AI.XII.F.K6	Simulated propeller feathering and the evaluator's zero-thrust procedures and responsibilities.
AI.XII.F.K7	Common errors related to this Task.

Risk Management:	The applicant explains and teaches how to identify and manage risk associated with:
AI.XII.F.R1	Potential engine failure after lift-off.
AI.XII.F.R2	Collision hazards.
AI.XII.F.R3	Configuring the airplane.
AI.XII.F.R4	Low altitude maneuvering, including stall, spin, or controlled flight into terrain (CFIT).
AI.XII.F.R5	Distractions, task prioritization, loss of situational awareness, or disorientation.

Skills:	The applicant demonstrates and simultaneously explains how to:
AI.XII.F.S1	Promptly recognize an engine failure, maintain control, and use appropriate emergency procedures.
AI.XII.F.S2	Establish V_{YSE}; if obstructions are present, establish best single-engine angle of climb speed (V_{XSE}) or V_{MC} +5 knots, whichever is greater, until obstructions are cleared. Then transition to V_{YSE}.
AI.XII.F.S3	Reduce drag by retracting landing gear and flaps in accordance with the manufacturer's guidance.
AI.XII.F.S4	Simulate feathering the propeller on the inoperative engine (evaluator should then establish zero thrust on the inoperative engine).
AI.XII.F.S5	Use flight controls in the proper combination as recommended by the manufacturer, or as required to maintain best performance, and trim as required.
AI.XII.F.S6	Monitor the operating engine and aircraft systems and make adjustments as necessary.

AI.XII.F.S7	Recognize the airplane's performance capabilities. If a climb is not possible at V_{YSE}, maintain V_{YSE} and return to the departure airport for landing, or initiate an approach to the most suitable landing area available.
AI.XII.F.S8	Simulate securing the inoperative engine.
AI.XII.F.S9	Maintain heading ±10° and airspeed ±5 knots.
AI.XII.F.S10	Complete the appropriate checklist(s).
AI.XII.F.S11	Analyze and correct common errors related to this Task.

Task G. Approach and Landing with an Inoperative Engine (Simulated) (AMEL, AMES)

References: FAA-H-8083-2, FAA-H-8083-3, FAA-H-8083-9, FAA-H-8083-25; FAA-P-8740-66; POH/AFM

Objective: To determine the applicant understands approach and landing with an inoperative engine, can apply that knowledge, manage associated risks, demonstrate appropriate skills, and provide effective instruction.

Note: See Appendix 2: Safety of Flight and Appendix 3: Aircraft, Equipment, and Operational Requirements & Limitations for information related to this Task.

Knowledge:	The applicant demonstrates instructional knowledge by describing and explaining:
AI.XII.G.K1	Factors affecting minimum controllable speed (V_{MC}).
AI.XII.G.K2	V_{MC} (red line) and best single-engine rate of climb airspeed (V_{YSE}) (blue line).
AI.XII.G.K3	How to identify, verify, feather, and secure an inoperative engine.
AI.XII.G.K4	Importance of drag reduction, including propeller feathering, gear and flap retraction, the manufacturer's recommended control input and its relation to zero sideslip.
AI.XII.G.K5	Applicant responsibilities during simulated feathering.
AI.XII.G.K6	Common errors related to this Task.

Risk Management:	The applicant explains and teaches how to identify and manage risk associated with:
AI.XII.G.R1	Potential engine failure after in flight or during an approach.
AI.XII.G.R2	Collision hazards.
AI.XII.G.R3	Configuring the airplane.
AI.XII.G.R4	Low altitude maneuvering, including stall, spin, or controlled flight into terrain (CFIT).
AI.XII.G.R5	Distractions, task prioritization, loss of situational awareness, or disorientation.
AI.XII.G.R6	Possible single-engine go-around.

Skills:	The applicant demonstrates and simultaneously explains how to:
AI.XII.G.S1	Promptly recognize an engine failure and maintain positive aircraft control.
AI.XII.G.S2	Set the engine controls, reduce drag, identify and verify the inoperative engine, and simulate feathering of the propeller on the inoperative engine (evaluator should then establish zero thrust on the inoperative engine).
AI.XII.G.S3	Follow the manufacturer's recommended emergency procedures and complete the appropriate checklist.
AI.XII.G.S4	Monitor the operating engine and aircraft systems and make adjustments as necessary.

AI.XII.G.S5	Maintain the manufacturer's recommended approach airspeed ±5 knots in the landing configuration with a stabilized approach, until landing is assured.
AI.XII.G.S6	Make smooth, timely, and correct control application before, during, and after touchdown.
AI.XII.G.S7	Touch down on the first one-third of available runway/landing surface, with no drift, and the airplane's longitudinal axis aligned with and over the runway center or landing path.
AI.XII.G.S8	Maintain directional control and appropriate crosswind correction throughout the approach and landing.
AI.XII.G.S9	Complete the appropriate checklist(s).
AI.XII.G.S10	Analyze and correct common errors related to this Task.

Area of Operation XIII. Multiengine Operations

Note: The evaluator must assess all Tasks.

Task A. Maneuvering with One Engine Inoperative (AMEL, AMES)

References: FAA-H-8083-2, FAA-H-8083-3, FAA-H-8083-9, FAA-H-8083-25; FAA-P-8740-66; POH/AFM

Objective: To determine the applicant understands one engine inoperative, can apply that knowledge, manage associated risks, demonstrate appropriate skills, and provide effective instruction.

Note: See Appendix 2: Safety of Flight.

Knowledge:	The applicant demonstrates instructional knowledge by describing and explaining:
AI.XIII.A.K1	Factors affecting minimum controllable speed (V_{MC}).
AI.XIII.A.K2	V_{MC} (red line) and best single-engine rate of climb airspeed (V_{YSE}) (blue line).
AI.XIII.A.K3	How to identify, verify, feather, and secure an inoperative engine.
AI.XIII.A.K4	Importance of drag reduction, including propeller feathering, gear and flap retraction, the manufacturer's recommended control input and its relation to zero sideslip.
AI.XIII.A.K5	Feathering, securing, unfeathering, and restarting.
AI.XIII.A.K6	Common errors related to this Task.

Risk Management:	The applicant explains and teaches how to identify and manage risk associated with:
AI.XIII.A.R1	Potential engine failure during flight.
AI.XIII.A.R2	Collision hazards.
AI.XIII.A.R3	Configuring the airplane.
AI.XIII.A.R4	Low altitude maneuvering, including stall, spin, or controlled flight into terrain (CFIT).
AI.XIII.A.R5	Distractions, task prioritization, loss of situational awareness, or disorientation.

Skills:	The applicant demonstrates and simultaneously explains how to:
AI.XIII.A.S1	Recognize an engine failure, maintain control, use manufacturer's memory item procedures, and use appropriate emergency procedures.
AI.XIII.A.S2	Set the engine controls, identify and verify the inoperative engine, and feather the appropriate propeller.
AI.XIII.A.S3	Use flight controls in the proper combination as recommended by the manufacturer, or as required to maintain best performance, and trim as required.
AI.XIII.A.S4	Attempt to determine and resolve the reason for the engine failure.
AI.XIII.A.S5	Secure the inoperative engine and monitor the operating engine and make necessary adjustments.
AI.XIII.A.S6	Restart the inoperative engine using manufacturer's restart procedures.
AI.XIII.A.S7	Maintain altitude ±100 feet or minimum sink rate if applicable, airspeed ±10 knots, and selected headings ±10°.
AI.XIII.A.S8	Complete the appropriate checklist(s).
AI.XIII.A.S9	Analyze and correct common errors related to this Task.

Task B. V_{MC} Demonstration (AMEL, AMES)

References: *FAA-H-8083-2, FAA-H-8083-3, FAA-H-8083-9, FAA-H-8083-25; FAA-P-8740-66; POH/AFM*

Objective: To determine the applicant understands V_{MC} demonstration, can apply that knowledge, manage associated risks, demonstrate appropriate skills, and provide effective instruction.

Note: *See Appendix 2: Safety of Flight and Appendix 3: Aircraft, Equipment, and Operational Requirements & Limitations for information related to this Task.*

Knowledge:	The applicant demonstrates instructional knowledge by describing and explaining:
AI.XIII.B.K1	Purpose of the maneuver.
AI.XIII.B.K2	Proper procedures for maneuver entry and safe recovery.
AI.XIII.B.K3	Factors affecting V_{MC} and how V_{MC} differs from stall speed (V_S).
AI.XIII.B.K4	V_{MC} (red line), V_{YSE} (blue line), and safe single-engine speed (V_{SSE}).
AI.XIII.B.K5	Cause of loss of directional control at airspeeds below V_{MC}.
AI.XIII.B.K6	Common errors related to this Task.

Risk Management:	The applicant explains and teaches how to identify and manage risk associated with:
AI.XIII.B.R1	Configuring the airplane.
AI.XIII.B.R2	Maneuvering with one engine inoperative.
AI.XIII.B.R3	Distractions, task prioritization, loss of situational awareness, or disorientation.

Skills:	The applicant demonstrates and simultaneously explains how to:
AI.XIII.B.S1	Configure the airplane in accordance with the manufacturer's recommendations, in the absence of the manufacturer's recommendations, then at safe single-engine speed (V_{SSE}/V_{YSE}), as appropriate, and:
AI.XIII.B.S1a	a. Landing gear retracted
AI.XIII.B.S1b	b. Flaps set for takeoff
AI.XIII.B.S1c	c. Cowl flaps set for takeoff
AI.XIII.B.S1d	d. Trim set for takeoff
AI.XIII.B.S1e	e. Propellers set for high revolutions per minute (rpm)
AI.XIII.B.S1f	f. Power on critical engine reduced to idle and propeller windmilling
AI.XIII.B.S1g	g. Power on operating engine set to takeoff or maximum available power
AI.XIII.B.S2	Establish a single-engine climb attitude with the airspeed at approximately 10 knots above V_{SSE}.
AI.XIII.B.S3	Establish a bank angle not to exceed 5° toward the operating engine, as required for best performance and controllability.
AI.XIII.B.S4	Increase the pitch attitude slowly to reduce the airspeed at approximately 1 knot per second while applying increased rudder pressure as needed to maintain directional control.
AI.XIII.B.S5	Recognize and recover at the first indication of loss of directional control, stall warning, or buffet.
AI.XIII.B.S6	Recover promptly by simultaneously reducing power sufficiently on the operating engine, decreasing the angle of attack as necessary to regain airspeed and directional control, and without adding power on the simulated failed engine.

Al.XIII.B.S7	Recover within 20° of entry heading.
Al.XIII.B.S8	Advance power smoothly on the operating engine and accelerate to V_{SSE}/V_{YSE}, as appropriate, ±5 knots during recovery.
Al.XIII.B.S9	Analyze and correct common errors related to this Task.

Task C. Demonstration of Effects of Various Airspeeds and Configurations during Engine Inoperative Performance (AMEL and AMES)

References: FAA-H-8083-2, FAA-H-8083-3, FAA-H-8083-9, FAA-H-8083-25; FAA-P-8740-66; POH/AFM

Objective: To determine the applicant understands the effects of various airspeeds and configurations during engine inoperative performance, can apply that knowledge, manage associated risks, demonstrate appropriate skills, and provide effective instruction.

Note: See Appendix 2: Safety of Flight and Appendix 3: Aircraft, Equipment, and Operational Requirements & Limitations for information related to this Task.

Knowledge:	The applicant demonstrates instructional knowledge by describing and explaining:
Al.XIII.C.K1	Purpose for and elements of demonstration of effects of various airspeeds and configurations during engine inoperative performance.
Al.XIII.C.K2	Selection of appropriate altitude for the demonstration.
Al.XIII.C.K3	Proper entry procedure to include pitch attitude, bank attitude, and airspeed.
Al.XIII.C.K4	Effects on performance of airspeed changes at, above, and below V_{YSE}.
Al.XIII.C.K5	Effects on performance of various configurations including:
Al.XIII.C.K5a	a. Landing gear extended
Al.XIII.C.K5b	b. Wing flaps extended
Al.XIII.C.K5c	c. Landing gear and wing flaps extended
Al.XIII.C.K5d	d. Windmilling propeller on the inoperative engine
Al.XIII.C.K6	Airspeed control throughout the demonstration.
Al.XIII.C.K7	Smooth control technique and coordination throughout the demonstration.
Al.XIII.C.K8	Common errors related to this Task.

Risk Management:	The applicant explains and teaches how to identify and manage risk associated with:
Al.XIII.C.R1	Altitude selection.
Al.XIII.C.R2	Entry and recovery procedures.
Al.XIII.C.R3	Loss of control or stall.
Al.XIII.C.R4	Configuring the airplane.
Al.XIII.C.R5	Collision hazards.
Al.XIII.C.R6	Distractions, task prioritization, loss of situational awareness, or disorientation.

Skills:	The applicant demonstrates and simultaneously explains how to:
Al.XIII.C.S1	Demonstrate, describe, and explain effects of various airspeeds and configurations during engine inoperative performance.

AI.XIII.C.S2   Demonstrate smooth control inputs when transitioning between various airspeeds and configurations, which include:

AI.XIII.C.S2a   a. Landing gear extended

AI.XIII.C.S2b   b. Wing flaps extended

AI.XIII.C.S2c   c. Landing gear and wing flaps extended

AI.XIII.C.S2d   d. Windmilling propeller on the inoperative engine

AI.XIII.C.S3   Maintain appropriate airspeed, attitude, and altitude combinations for the various configurations.

AI.XIII.C.S4   Return to normal cruise flight at the altitude and heading specified by the evaluator.

AI.XIII.C.S5   Analyze and correct common errors related to this Task.

Area of Operation XIV. Postflight Procedures

Note: *The evaluator must select Task A (ASEL, AMEL) or Task B (ASES, AMES).*

Task A. After Landing, Parking, and Securing (ASEL, AMEL)

References: *FAA-H-8083-2, FAA-H-8083-3, FAA-H-8083-9, FAA-H-8083-25; POH/AFM*

Objective: To determine the applicant understands after landing, parking, and securing procedures, can apply that knowledge, manage associated risks, demonstrate appropriate skills, and provide effective instruction.

Knowledge:	The applicant demonstrates instructional knowledge by describing and explaining:
AI.XIV.A.K1	Airplane shutdown, securing, and postflight inspection.
AI.XIV.A.K2	Documenting in-flight/postflight discrepancies.
AI.XIV.A.K3	Common errors related to this Task.

Risk Management:	The applicant explains and teaches how to identify and manage risk associated with:
AI.XIV.A.R1	Activities and distractions.
AI.XIV.A.R2	Airport specific security procedures.
AI.XIV.A.R3	Disembarking passengers safely on the ramp and monitoring passenger movement while on the ramp.

Skills:	The applicant demonstrates and simultaneously explains how to:
AI.XIV.A.S1	Park in an appropriate area, considering the safety of nearby persons and property.
AI.XIV.A.S2	Complete the appropriate checklist(s).
AI.XIV.A.S3	Conduct a postflight inspection and document discrepancies and servicing requirements, if any.
AI.XIV.A.S4	Secure the airplane.
AI.XIV.A.S5	Analyze and correct common errors related to this Task.

Task B. Seaplane Post-Landing Procedures (ASES, AMES)

References: *FAA-H-8083-2, FAA-H-8083-9, FAA-H-8083-23, FAA-H-8083-25; POH/AFM*

Objective: To determine the applicant understands anchoring, docking, mooring, and ramping/beaching, can apply that knowledge, manage associated risks, demonstrate appropriate skills, and provide effective instruction.

Knowledge:	The applicant demonstrates instructional knowledge by describing and explaining:
AI.XIV.B.K1	Mooring.
AI.XIV.B.K2	Docking.
AI.XIV.B.K3	Anchoring.
AI.XIV.B.K4	Beaching/ramping.
AI.XIV.B.K5	Postflight inspection, recording of in-flight/postflight discrepancies.

AI.XIV.B.K6   Common errors related to this Task.

Risk
Management: The applicant explains and teaches how to identify and manage risk associated with:

AI.XIV.B.R1   Activities and distractions.

AI.XIV.B.R2   Seaplane base specific security procedures, if applicable.

AI.XIV.B.R3   Disembarking passengers safely on the ramp and monitoring passenger movement while on the ramp.

Skills: The applicant demonstrates and simultaneously explains how to:

AI.XIV.B.S1   If anchoring, select a suitable area considering seaplane movement, water depth, tide, wind, and weather changes. Use an adequate number of anchors and lines of sufficient strength and length to ensure the seaplane's security.

AI.XIV.B.S2   If not anchoring, approach the dock/mooring buoy or beach/ramp in the proper direction and at a safe speed, considering water depth, tide, current, and wind.

AI.XIV.B.S3   Complete the appropriate checklist(s).

AI.XIV.B.S4   Conduct a postflight inspection and document discrepancies and servicing requirements, if any.

AI.XIV.B.S5   Secure the seaplane considering the effect of wind, waves, and changes in water level, or comply with applicable after landing, parking, and securing procedures if operating an amphibious airplane on land.

AI.XIV.B.S6   Analyze and correct common errors related to this Task.

Appendix 1: Practical Test Roles, Responsibilities, and Outcomes

Eligibility Requirements for a Flight Instructor Certificate

The prerequisite requirements and general eligibility for a practical test and the specific requirements for the issuance of a Flight Instructor Certificate in the airplane category can be found in 14 CFR part 61, sections 61.39(a) and 61.183.

In accordance with 14 CFR part 61, section 61.39, the applicant must pass the airman knowledge test before taking the practical test, if applicable to the certificate or rating sought.

For an initial flight instructor certificate or when adding the airplane category to an existing flight instructor certificate, applicants must pass the knowledge test listed in the table below as a prerequisite for the practical test.

Test Code	Test Name	Number of Questions	Age	Allotted Time	Passing Score
FOI*	Fundamentals of Instructing	50	16	1.5	70
FIA	Flight Instructor – Airplane	100	16	2.5	70
AFA	Flight Instructor – Airplane (Added Rating)	25	16	1.0	70

*The FOI knowledge test applies unless the applicant meets the criteria listed in 14 CFR part 61, section 61.183(e).

Use of the ACS During a Practical Test

The practical test is conducted in accordance with the ACS and FAA regulations that are current as of the date of the test.

The Areas of Operation in this ACS align with the Areas of Operation found in 14 CFR part 61, section 61.187(b). Each Area of Operation includes Tasks appropriate to that Area of Operation. Each Task contains an Objective stating what the applicant must know, consider, and/or do. The ACS then lists the aeronautical knowledge, risk management, and skill elements relevant to the specific Task, along with the conditions and standards for acceptable performance. The ACS uses Notes to emphasize special considerations.

During the ground and flight portion of the practical test, the FAA expects evaluators to assess the applicant's mastery of the topic in accordance with the level of learning most appropriate for the specified Task. The oral questioning will continue throughout the entire practical test. For some topics, the evaluator will ask the applicant to describe or explain. For other items, the evaluator will assess the applicant's understanding by providing a scenario that requires the applicant to appropriately apply and/or correlate knowledge, experience, and information to the circumstances of the given scenario. The flight portion of the practical test requires the applicant to demonstrate knowledge, risk management, flight proficiency, and operational skill in accordance with the ACS.

The elements within each Task in this ACS are coded according to a scheme that includes four components. For example, FI.I.C.K2:

> FI = Applicable ACS
>
> I = Area of Operation
>
> C = Task
>
> K2 = Task element (in this example, Knowledge 2)

There is no requirement for an evaluator to test every knowledge and risk management element in a Task; rather the evaluator has discretion to sample as needed to ensure the applicant's mastery of that Task. The required minimum elements to be tested from each applicable Task include:

- any elements in which the applicant was shown to be deficient on the knowledge test, as applicable;
- at least one knowledge element;
- at least one risk management element; and
- all skill elements unless otherwise noted.

The Airman Knowledge Test Report (AKTR) lists ACS codes that correlate to a specific Task element for a given Area of Operation for any incorrect responses on the knowledge test.

Knowledge and risk management elements are primarily evaluated during the knowledge testing phase of the airman certification process. The evaluator administering the practical test has the discretion to combine Tasks/elements as appropriate to testing scenarios.

Unless otherwise noted in the Task, the evaluator must test each item in the skills section by observing the applicant perform each one. As safety of flight conditions permit, the evaluator should use questions during flight to test knowledge and risk management elements not evident in the demonstrated skills. To the greatest extent practicable, evaluators should test the applicant's ability to apply and correlate information and use rote questions only when they are appropriate for the material being tested.

If the Task includes a knowledge or risk element with sub-elements, the evaluator may choose the primary element and select at least one sub-element to satisfy the requirement. Selection of the sub-element satisfies the requirement for one element unless otherwise noted.

For example, an evaluator who chooses FI.I.F.K2 may select a sub-element such as FI.I.F.K2b to satisfy the requirement to select one knowledge element.

The References for each Task indicate the source material for Task elements. For example, in the Task element "Acceptable weather products and resources required for preflight planning, current and forecast weather for departure, en route, and arrival phases of flight such as:" (AI.III.C.K2), the applicant should be prepared for questions on any weather product presented in the references for that Task.

> **Note:** *When administering a test, the Tasks appropriate to the class airplane (ASEL, ASES, AMEL, or AMES) used for the test must be included in the plan of action.*

The FAA encourages applicants and instructors to use the ACS when preparing for the airman knowledge tests and practical tests. Evaluators must conduct the practical test in accordance with the current ACS and FAA regulations pursuant to 14 CFR part 61, section 61.43. If an applicant is entitled to credit for Areas of Operation previously passed as indicated on a Notice of Disapproval of Application or Letter of Discontinuance, evaluators shall use the ACS currently in effect on the date of the test.

The ground portion of the practical test allows the evaluator to determine whether the applicant is sufficiently prepared to advance to the flight portion of the practical test. The applicant must pass the ground portion of the practical test before beginning the flight portion. The oral questioning will continue throughout the entire practical test.

Instructor Responsibilities

The instructor trains and qualifies the applicant to meet the established standards for knowledge, risk management, and skill elements in all Tasks appropriate to the certificate and rating sought. The instructor should use this ACS and its references when preparing the applicant to take the practical test and when retraining the applicant to proficiency in any subject(s) missed on the knowledge test.

Evaluator Responsibilities

An evaluator includes the following:

- Aviation Safety Inspector (ASI);
- Pilot examiner (other than administrative pilot examiners);
- Training center evaluator (TCE);
- Chief instructor, assistant chief instructor, or check instructor of pilot school holding examining authority; or
- Instrument Flight Instructor (CFII) conducting an instrument proficiency check (IPC).

The evaluator who conducts the practical test verifies the applicant has met the aeronautical experience requirements specified for a certificate or rating before administering the test. During the practical test, the evaluator determines whether the applicant meets the established standards of aeronautical knowledge, risk management, and skills for the Tasks in the appropriate ACS.

The evaluator must develop a plan of action (POA) that includes all required Areas of Operation and Tasks and administer each practical test in English. The POA must include scenario(s) that evaluate as many of the required Areas of Operation and Tasks as possible. As a scenario unfolds during the test, the evaluator will introduce problems and simulate emergencies that test the applicant's ability. The evaluator has the discretion to modify the POA to accommodate unexpected situations as they arise or suspend and later resume a scenario to assess certain Tasks.

Prior to and throughout the evaluation, the evaluator ensures the applicant meets the FAA Aviation English Language Standard (AELS). An applicant must be able to communicate in English in a discernible and understandable manner with air traffic control (ATC), pilots, and others involved in preparing an aircraft for flight and operating an aircraft in flight. This communication may or may not involve radio communications. An applicant for an FAA certificate or rating issued in accordance with 14 CFR parts 61, 63, 65, or 107 who cannot hear or speak due to a medical deficiency may be eligible for an FAA certificate with specific operational limitations.

If the applicant's ability to meet the FAA AELS comes into question before starting the practical test, the evaluator will not begin the practical test. An evaluator other than an ASI will check the box, "Referred to FSO for Aviation English Language Standard Determination," located on the bottom of page 2 of the applicant's FAA Form 8710-1, Airman Certificate and/or Rating Application, or FAA Form 8710-11, Airman Certificate and/or Rating Application - Sport Pilot, as applicable. The evaluator will refer the applicant to the appropriate Flight Standards Office (FSO).

If the applicant's ability to meet the FAA AELS comes into question after the practical test begins, an evaluator who other than an ASI will discontinue the practical test and check the box, "Referred to FSO for Aviation English Language Standard Determination," on the application. The evaluator will also issue FAA Form 8060-5, Notice of Disapproval of Application, with the comment "Does Not Demonstrate FAA AELS" in addition to any unsatisfactory Task(s). The evaluator will refer the applicant to the appropriate FSO. ASIs conducting the practical test may assess an applicant's English language proficiency in accordance with FAA Order 8900.1.

In either case, the evaluator must complete and submit the application file through normal application procedures and evaluators other than an ASI notify the appropriate FSO of the referral.

If the ability of an FAA certificated airman comes into question prior to or during a required regulatory check (e.g., proficiency check) the evaluator other than an ASI will not continue the check or provide an endorsement indicating completion. The evaluator will refer the airman to the jurisdictional FAA field office for further determination of ability to meet the FAA AELS.

For additional information, reference AC 60-28, FAA English Language Standard for an FAA Certificate issued under 14 CFR parts 61, 63, 65, and 107, as amended.

The abbreviation(s) within parentheses immediately following a Task refers to the category and/or class airplane appropriate to that Task. The absence of a class indicates the Task is for all classes. The meaning of each abbreviation is as follows:

- ASEL—Airplane – Single-Engine Land
- ASES—Airplane – Single-Engine Sea
- AMEL—Airplane – Multiengine Land
- AMES—Airplane – Multiengine Sea

The evaluator conducting the practical test must determine that the applicant meets acceptable standards of teaching ability in the selected Tasks. The evaluator makes this determination by confirming the applicant's:

- Ability to apply the fundamentals of instructing;
- Knowledge of and ability to teach the subject matter, procedures, and maneuvers covered in the Tasks;
- Ability to perform the Tasks at the level of a commercial pilot while giving effective flight instruction; and
- Ability to analyze and correct common errors related to the procedures and maneuvers covered in the Tasks.

During the flight portion of the practical test, the evaluator may act as a student during selected maneuvers. This gives the evaluator an opportunity to evaluate the flight instructor applicant's ability to analyze and correct simulated common errors related to these maneuvers.

Possible Outcomes of the Test

A practical test has three possible outcomes: (1) Temporary Airman Certificate (satisfactory), (2) Notice of Disapproval of Application (unsatisfactory), or (3) Letter of Discontinuance.

If the evaluator determines that a Task is incomplete, or the outcome is uncertain, the evaluator must require the applicant to repeat that Task, or portions of that Task. This provision does not mean that instruction, practice, or the repetition of an unsatisfactory Task is permitted during the practical test.

Satisfactory Performance

Refer to 14 CFR part 61, section 61.43, for satisfactory performance requirements.

Satisfactory performance will result in the issuance of a temporary certificate.

Unsatisfactory Performance

If, in the judgment of the evaluator, the applicant does not meet the standards for any Task, the applicant fails the Task and associated Area of Operation and the evaluator issues a Notice of Disapproval of Application. The evaluator lists the Area(s) of Operation in which the applicant did not meet the standard, any Area(s) of Operation not tested, and the number of practical test failures. The evaluator should also list the Tasks failed or Tasks not tested within any unsatisfactory or partially completed Area(s) of Operation. 14 CFR part 61, section 61.43(c)–(f) provides additional unsatisfactory performance requirements and parameters.

Typical areas of unsatisfactory performance and grounds for disqualification include:

- Any action or lack of action by the applicant that requires corrective intervention by the evaluator to maintain safe flight.
- Failure to use proper and effective visual scanning techniques to clear the area before and while performing maneuvers.
- Consistently exceeding tolerances stated in the skill elements of the Task.
- Failure to take prompt corrective action when tolerances are exceeded.
- Failure to exercise risk management.
- Failure to provide effective instruction while demonstrating a procedure or maneuver.

The evaluator or the applicant may end the test if the applicant fails a Task. The evaluator may continue the test only with the consent of the applicant. The applicant receives credit only for those Areas of Operation and the associated Tasks performed satisfactorily.

Letter of Discontinuance

Refer to 14 CFR part 61, section 61.43(e)(2) for conditions to issue a letter of discontinuance.

If discontinuing a practical test for reasons other than unsatisfactory performance (e.g., equipment failure, weather, illness), the evaluator must return all test paperwork to the applicant. The evaluator must prepare, sign, and issue a Letter of Discontinuance that lists those Areas of Operation the applicant successfully completed and the time period remaining to complete the test to receive credit for previously completed Areas of Operation. The evaluator should advise the applicant to present the Letter of Discontinuance to the evaluator when the practical test resumes in order to receive credit for the items successfully completed. The Letter of Discontinuance becomes part of the applicant's certification file.

Time Limit and Credit after a Discontinued Practical Test

Refer to 14 CFR part 61, sections 61.39(f) and 61.43(f) after issuance of a Letter of Discontinuance or Notice of Disapproval of Application.

Additional Rating Task Table

For an applicant who holds a Flight Instructor Certificate and seeks an additional Airplane category and/or class rating at the Flight Instructor level, the evaluator must evaluate that applicant in the Areas of Operation and Tasks listed in the Additional Rating Task Table. The evaluator may evaluate the applicant's competence in the remaining Areas of Operation and Tasks.

If the applicant holds two or more category or class ratings at the flight instructor level, and the ratings table indicates different Task requirements, the least restrictive entry applies. For example, if an asterisk (*) and "None" are indicated for one Area of Operation, the "None" entry applies. If the table indicates "B" and "B, C" the "B" entry applies.

Addition of an Airplane Single-Engine Rating to an Existing Flight Instructor Certificate

The table below indicates the required Tasks for each Area of Operation tested in accordance with this ACS.

Legend	
AME	Airplane – Multiengine
RH	Rotorcraft – Helicopter
RG	Rotorcraft – Gyroplane
PL	Powered-Lift
IA	Instrument Rating – Airplane
IH	Instrument Rating – Helicopter
IP	Instrument Rating – Powered-Lift

Area of Operation	Flight Instructor Certificate and Rating(s) Held							
	AME	RH	RG	PL	Glider	IA	IH	IP
I	None	None	None	None	None	None	None	None
II	C,K	*	*	*	*	*	*	*
III	None	B	B	B	B	*	*	*
IV	None	None	None	None	None	None	None	None
V	None	*	*	*	*	*	*	*
VI	None	*	None	None	*	*	*	*
VII	*	*	*	*	*	*	*	*
VIII	None	*	*	None	*	*	*	*
IX	B and F, C or D	*	*	B and F, C or D	*	*	*	*
X	*	*	*	*	*	*	*	*
XI	None	*	*	None	*	None	*	None
XII	*	*	*	*	*	*	*	*
XIII	None	None	None	None	None	None	None	None
XIV	None	*	*	*	*	*	*	*

Note: *An asterisk directs the evaluator to refer to the Note under the respective Area of Operation for Task requirements.*

Addition of an Airplane Multiengine Rating to an Existing Flight Instructor Certificate

The table below indicates the required Tasks for each Area of Operation tested in accordance with this ACS.

Legend	
ASE	Airplane – Single-Engine
RH	Rotorcraft – Helicopter
RG	Rotorcraft – Gyroplane
PL	Powered-Lift
IA	Instrument Rating – Airplane
IH	Instrument Rating – Helicopter
IP	Instrument Rating – Powered-Lift

Area of Operation	Flight Instructor Certificate and Rating(s) Held							
	ASE	RH	RG	PL	Glider	IA	IH	IP
I	None	None	None	None	None	None	None	None
II	C,K,P	*	*	*	*	*	*	*
III	None	B	B	B	B	*	*	*
IV	None	None	None	None	None	None	None	None
V	*	*	*	*	*	*	*	*
VI	None	*	None	None	*	*	*	*
VII	*	*	*	*	*	*	*	*
VIII	None	*	*	None	*	*	*	*
IX	A	*	*	A	*	*	*	*
X	*	*	*	*	*	*	*	*
XI	None	*	*	None	*	None	*	None
XII	*	*	*	*	*	*	*	*
XIII	*	*	*	*	*	*	*	*
XIV	None	*	*	*	*	*	*	*

Note: *An asterisk directs the evaluator to refer to the Note under the respective Area of Operation for Task requirements.*

Flight Instructor Renewal/Reinstatement

In accordance with 14 CFR part 61, section 61.199(a), the renewal or reinstatement of one rating on a Flight Instructor Certificate renews or reinstates all privileges existing on the certificate.

Required Area of Operation	Airplane Single-Engine	Airplane Multiengine
I	**	**
II	C,K, and 1 other Task	C,K,P, and 1 other Task
III	1 Task	1 Task
IV	1 Task	1 Task
V	1 Task	1 Task
VI	None	None
VII	2 Takeoffs 2 Landings	2 Takeoffs 2 Landings
VIII	None	None
IX	Ground Reference - 1 Task Performance - 1 Task	Ground Reference - 1 Task Performance - 1 Task
X	2 Tasks	1 Task
XI	None	None
XII	1 Task	2 Tasks
XIII	None	1 Task
XIV	1 Task	1 Task

Note: *A double asterisk directs the evaluator to consider the period of inactivity. The evaluator may test FOI Tasks for any reinstatement.*

Appendix 2: Safety of Flight

General

Safety of flight must be the prime consideration at all times. The evaluator, applicant, and crew must be continually alert for other traffic. If performing aspects of a given maneuver, such as emergency procedures, would jeopardize safety, the evaluator will ask the applicant to simulate that portion of the maneuver. The evaluator will assess the applicant's use of visual scanning and collision avoidance procedures throughout the entire test.

Stall and Spin Awareness

During flight training and testing, the applicant and the instructor or evaluator must always recognize and avoid operations that could lead to an inadvertent stall or spin and inadvertent loss of control.

Use of Checklists

Throughout the practical test, the applicant is evaluated on the use of an appropriate checklist.

Assessing proper checklist use depends upon the specific Task. In all cases, the evaluator should determine whether the applicant demonstrates CRM, appropriately divides attention, and uses proper visual scanning. In some situations, reading the actual checklist may be impractical or unsafe. In such cases, the evaluator should assess the applicant's performance of published or recommended immediate action "memory" items along with their review of the appropriate checklist once conditions permit.

In a single-pilot aircraft, the applicant should demonstrate the crew resource management (CRM) principles described as single-pilot resource management (SRM). Proper use depends on the specific Task being evaluated. If the use of the checklist while accomplishing elements of an Objective would be either unsafe or impractical in a single-pilot operation, the applicant should review the checklist after accomplishing the elements.

Positive Exchange of Flight Controls

A clear understanding of who has control of the aircraft must exist. Prior to flight, the pilots involved should conduct a briefing that includes reviewing the procedures for exchanging flight controls.

The FAA recommends a positive three-step process for exchanging flight controls between pilots:

- When one pilot seeks to have the other pilot take control of the aircraft, they will say, "You have the flight controls."
- The second pilot acknowledges immediately by saying, "I have the flight controls."
- The first pilot again says, "You have the flight controls," and visually confirms the exchange.

Pilots should follow this procedure during any exchange of flight controls, including any occurrence during the practical test. The FAA also recommends that both pilots use a visual check to verify that the exchange has occurred. Doubt as to who is flying the aircraft should not occur.

Use of Distractions

Numerous studies indicate that many accidents have occurred when the pilot has been distracted during critical phases of flight. The evaluator should incorporate realistic distractions during the flight portion of the practical test to evaluate the pilot's situational awareness and ability to utilize proper control technique while dividing attention both inside and outside the flight deck.

Aeronautical Decision-Making, Risk Management, Crew Resource Management, and Single-Pilot Resource Management

Throughout the practical test, the evaluator must assess the applicant's ability to use sound aeronautical decision-making procedures in order to identify hazards and mitigate risk. The evaluator must accomplish this requirement by reference to the risk management elements of the given Task(s), and by developing scenarios that incorporate and combine Tasks appropriate to assessing the applicant's risk management in making safe aeronautical decisions. For example, the evaluator may develop a scenario that incorporates weather decisions and performance planning.

In assessing the applicant's performance, the evaluator should take note of the applicant's use of CRM and, if appropriate, SRM. CRM/SRM is the set of competencies that includes situational awareness, communication skills, teamwork, task allocation, and decision-making within a comprehensive framework of standard operating procedures (SOP). SRM specifically refers to the management of all resources onboard the aircraft, as well as outside resources available to the single pilot.

If an applicant fails to use aeronautical decision-making (ADM), including SRM/CRM, as applicable in any Task, the evaluator will note that Task as failed. The evaluator will also include the ADM Skill element from the Flight Deck Management Task on the Notice of Disapproval of Application.

Multiengine Considerations

On multiengine practical tests, where the failure of the most critical engine after liftoff is required, the evaluator must consider local atmospheric conditions, terrain, and type of aircraft used. The evaluator must not simulate failure of an engine until attaining an altitude of at least 400 feet AGL and at least minimum single-engine speed (V_{SSE}), best single-engine angle-of-climb speed (V_{XSE}), or best single-engine rate-of-climb (V_{YSE}).

The applicant must supply an airplane that does not prohibit the demonstration of feathering the propeller in flight. However, an applicant holding an unrestricted AMEL rating may take a practical test for the addition of an AMES rating in an AMES without propeller feathering capability. Practical tests conducted in a flight simulation training device (FSTD) can only be accomplished as part of an approved curriculum or training program pursuant to 14 CFR part 61, section 61.64. Any limitations or powerplant failure will be noted in that program.

For safety reasons, when the practical test is conducted in an airplane, the applicant must perform Tasks that require feathering or shutdown only under conditions and at a position and altitude where it is possible to make a safe landing on an established airport if there is difficulty in unfeathering the propeller or restarting the engine. The evaluator must select an entry altitude that will allow the single-engine demonstration Tasks to be completed no lower than 3,000 feet AGL or the manufacturer's recommended altitude (whichever is higher). If it is not possible to unfeather the propeller or restart the engine while airborne, the applicant and the evaluator should treat the situation as an emergency. At altitudes lower than 3,000 feet AGL, engine failure should be simulated by reducing throttle to idle and then establishing zero thrust.

Engine failure (simulated) during takeoff should be accomplished prior to reaching 50 percent of the calculated V_{MC}.

Single-Engine Considerations

For safety reasons, the evaluator will not request a simulated powerplant failure in a single-engine airplane unless it is possible to safely complete a landing.

Appendix 3: Aircraft, Equipment, and Operational Requirements & Limitations

Aircraft Requirements & Limitations

If the aircraft has inoperative equipment and can be operated in accordance with 14 CFR part 91, section 91.213, it must be determined if any inoperative instruments or equipment are required to complete the practical test. The inoperative equipment must not interfere with practical test requirements.

Equipment Requirements & Limitations

The aircraft must meet the requirements as outlined in 14 CFR part 61, section 61.45.

To assist in management of the aircraft during the practical test, the applicant is expected to demonstrate automation management skills by utilizing installed, available, or airborne equipment such as autopilot, avionics and systems displays, and/or a flight management system (FMS). The evaluator is expected to test the applicant's knowledge of the systems that are available or installed and operative during both the ground and flight portions of the practical test. If the applicant has trained using a portable electronic flight bag (EFB) to display charts and data and wishes to use the EFB during the practical test, the applicant is expected to demonstrate appropriate knowledge, risk management, and skill appropriate to its use.

If the practical test involves maneuvering the aircraft solely by reference to instruments, the applicant is required by 14 CFR part 61, section 61.45(d)(2) to provide an appropriate view limiting device acceptable to the Administrator. The applicant and the evaluator should establish a procedure as to when and how this device should be donned and removed and brief this procedure before the flight. This device must prevent the applicant from having visual reference outside the aircraft, but it must not restrict the evaluator's ability to see and avoid other traffic. The use of the device does not apply to specific elements within a Task when there is a requirement for visual references.

Use of Flight Simulation Training Devices (FSTD)

Applicants for a pilot certificate or rating can accomplish all or part of a practical test or proficiency check in an FSTD qualified under 14 CFR part 60, which includes full flight simulators (FFS) or flight training devices (FTD), only when conducted within an FAA-approved training program. Each operational rule part identifies additional requirements for the approval and use of FSTDs in an FAA-approved training program.

Credit for Pilot Time in an FSTD

14 CFR part 61 and part 141 specify the minimum experience requirements for each certificate or rating sought. 14 CFR part 61 and the appendices to part 141 specify the maximum amount of FFS or FTD flight training time an applicant can apply toward those experience requirements.

Use of Aviation Training Devices (ATD)

Applicants for a pilot certificate or rating cannot use an ATD to accomplish a practical test, a 14 CFR part 61, section 61.58 proficiency check, or the flight portion of a 14 CFR part 61, section 61.57 flight review. An ATD is defined in 14 CFR part 61, section 61.1.

The FAA's General Aviation and Commercial Division evaluates and approves ATDs as permitted under 14 CFR part 61, section 61.4(c) and FAA Order 8900.1. Each ATD is then issued an FAA letter of authorization (LOA) that is valid for 60 calendar months. The LOA for each ATD lists the pilot time credit allowances and associated limitations.

The Pilot Training and Certification Group public website provides a list of the FAA-approved ATDs and the associated manufacturer.

Credit for Pilot Time in an ATD

14 CFR part 61 and part 141 specify the minimum experience requirements for each certificate or rating sought. 14 CFR part 61 and the appendices to part 141 specify the maximum amount of ATD flight training time an applicant can apply toward those experience requirements. The LOA for each FAA-approved ATD lists the pilot time credit allowances and the associated limitations.

Evaluators must request an applicant to provide a copy of the manufacturer's LOA when using ATD flight training time credit to meet the minimum experience requirements for an airman pilot certificate, rating, or privilege.

Operational Requirements, Limitations, & Task Information

VIII. Takeoffs, Landings, and Go-Arounds

Task M. Power-Off 180° Accuracy Approach and Landing (ASEL, ASES)

Note that certain single-engine turboprop airplanes experience an excessive rate of descent if the power is set to flight idle. In some cases, if the powerplant failed, the manufacturer's checklist calls for feathering the propeller during a power-off glide. During flight training in these airplanes, the propeller is not feathered as would be the case in an emergency or true power-off glide. During training and pilot certification, where the manufacturer's checklist calls for propeller feathering in a power-off situation, the pilot should set sufficient power to provide the performance that would be expected with the propeller feathered.

Initiating a go-around as a result of an applicant's inability to complete this Task within the tolerances specified in the skill elements is considered unsatisfactory. Runway safety concerns beyond the control of the applicant or evaluator that necessitate a go-around would not be considered unsatisfactory. The applicant and evaluator must not sacrifice the safety of flight and force a landing to complete this Task.

X. Slow Flight, Stalls, and Spins (Spins apply to ASEL)

Some stall Tasks allow for demonstration or teaching of full stalls. With the exception of Task H - Secondary Stalls (where a full stall occurs) and Task E - Accelerated Stall (where the recovery occurs at the first indication), the evaluator has discretion to ask for recovery at the first indication of a stall or after a full stall occurs. Applicants should train and prepare to demonstrate or teach full stalls where appropriate; however, the applicant and the evaluator must review this area of operation during the preflight briefing.

The flight instructor normally demonstrates stall Tasks F, G, and H to learners for the purposes of familiarization and stall/ spin awareness. Private and commercial pilot certification does not include these Tasks.

Task A. Maneuvering During Slow Flight and Task B. Demonstration of Flight Characteristics at Various Configurations and Airspeeds

Evaluation criteria for this Task should recognize that environmental factors (e.g., turbulence) may result in a momentary activation of stall warning indicators such as the stall horn. If the applicant recognizes the stall warning indication and promptly makes an appropriate correction, a momentary activation does not constitute unsatisfactory performance on this Task. As with other Tasks, unsatisfactory performance would arise from an applicant's continual deviation from the standard, lack of correction, and/or lack of recognition.

Task C. Power-Off Stalls

Evaluation criteria for a recovery from an approach to stall should not mandate a predetermined value for altitude loss and should not mandate maintaining altitude during recovery. Proper evaluation criteria should consider the multitude of external and internal variables that affect the recovery altitude.

Task D. Power-On Stalls

In some high-performance airplanes, the power setting may have to be reduced below the ACS guidelines power setting to prevent pitch attitudes greater than 30° nose up. Evaluation criteria for a recovery from an approach to stall does not mandate a predetermined value for altitude loss and does not mandate maintaining altitude during recovery. Proper evaluation criteria considers the multitude of external and internal variables that affect the recovery altitude.

Task E. Accelerated Stalls

Pilots must set power for airspeed at or below the design maneuvering speed (V_A) for the airplane. In a multiengine airplane a successful recovery occurs at the first indication of a stall. Delaying application of power until the airplane reaches a wings level altitude, attains a speed that exceeds V_{MC}, and responds normally to control inputs is acceptable. A pilot should delay application of high power if the aircraft is not above V_{MC} and responding as expected.

Evaluation criteria for a recovery from an approach to stall should not mandate a predetermined value for altitude loss and should not mandate maintaining altitude during recovery. Proper evaluation criteria should consider the multitude of external and internal variables that affect the recovery altitude.

Task G. Elevator Trim Stalls

The applicant and evaluator must brief the recovery prior to stall execution. A realistic scenario includes a simulated short-field approach at altitude trimmed for approach airspeed, low power, and full flaps.

Task H. Secondary Stalls

Secondary stalls include a full stall.

XII. Emergency Operations

Task B. Emergency Approach and Landing (Simulated) (ASEL, ASES)

Execution must allow for a safe landing in the event of an actual engine failure.

Task D. Emergency Equipment and Survival Gear

For airplanes that include a ballistic parachute, applicants must follow the manufacturer's procedures for arming and disarming the system before and after flight. Testing of an applicant's knowledge regarding how and when to use the system and how to manage associated risks may include simulation and briefing of procedures but not actual deployment of the system.

Task E. Engine Failure During Takeoff Before V_{MC} (Simulated) [Airplane, Multiengine Land (AMEL); Airplane, Multiengine Sea (AMES)]

Engine failure (simulated) during takeoff should be accomplished prior to reaching 50 percent of the calculated V_{MC}.

Task F. Engine Failure After Liftoff (Simulated) (AMEL, AMES)

The evaluator must not simulate failure of an engine until attaining an altitude of at least 400 feet AGL and at least minimum single-engine speed (V_{SSE}), best single-engine angle-of-climb speed (V_{XSE}), or best single-engine rate-of-climb (V_{YSE}).

Task G. Approach and Landing with an Inoperative Engine (Simulated) [Airplane, Multiengine Land (AMEL); Airplane, Multiengine See (AMES)]

For tests conducted in a propeller-driven airplane (other than those that require a type rating), the evaluator shall require the instructor applicant to simultaneously demonstrate and explain procedures for landing with a simulated feathered propeller with the engine set to zero thrust .

The applicant must simultaneously demonstrate and explain at least one landing with a simulated feathered propeller with the powerplant set to zero thrust. For all other airplanes, follow the manufacturer's recommended procedures.

XIII. Multiengine Operations

Airplanes with normally aspirated engines will lose power as altitude increases because of the reduced density of the air entering the induction system of the engine. This loss of power will result in a V_{MC} lower than the stall speed at higher altitudes. Therefore, recovery should be made at the first indication of loss of directional control, stall warning, or buffet. Do not perform this maneuver by increasing the pitch attitude to a high angle with both engines operating and then reducing power on the critical engine. This technique is hazardous and may result in loss of airplane control.

U.S. Department
of Transportation

**Federal Aviation
Administration**

FAA-G-ACS-2

Airman Certification Standards
Companion Guide for Pilots

November 2023

Flight Standards Service
Washington, DC 20591

Foreword

The Federal Aviation Administration (FAA) developed this Airman Certification Standards Companion Guide FAA-G-ACS-2, for use with the Airman Certification Standards (ACS) for pilot certification. This guide, along with the regulatory material in the ACS, may assist an applicant preparing for the knowledge and practical test(s) that lead to pilot certification. This document is intended only to provide clarity to the public regarding existing requirements under the law or agency policies. The contents of this document do not have the force and effect of law and are not meant to bind the public in any way.

This guide and the ACS are available for download from www.faa.gov.

Comments regarding this document may be emailed to acsptsinquiries@faa.gov.

Revision History

Document #	Description	Date
FAA-G-ACS-2	Airman Certification Standards Companion Guide for Pilots	November 2023

Table of Contents

Why the FAA Created this Guide

The Federal Aviation Administration (FAA) publishes the Airman Certification Standards (ACS) to communicate the aeronautical knowledge, risk management, and flight proficiency standards for various certificates and ratings available to airmen. The ACSs are incorporated by reference into 14 CFR part 61; therefore, the material contained in the ACS is regulatory. This guide, FAA-G-ACS-2, provides additional information to the regulated community to facilitate airman testing. The ACS complies with the safety management system (SMS) framework that the FAA uses to mitigate risks associated with airman certification training and testing. Specifically, the ACS, incorporated by reference (IBR) into the Federal Aviation Regulations, conforms to four functional components of an SMS:

- Safety Policy—Each ACS specifies the Tasks selected by the FAA from the regulatory Areas of Operation. Evaluators formulate a Plan of Action that determines if an applicant can operate safely within the NAS. The ACS represents the FAA's commitment to continually improve safety by including risk management elements in addition to knowledge and skill elements;

- Safety Risk Management that complies with the Administrative Procedures Act (APA) allows the FAA to work with internal and external stakeholders during document formulation. The public at large and stakeholders have an additional chance to provide input during public comment periods;

- Safety Assurance processes ensure a methodical and reasoned incorporation of changes arising from safety recommendations or new developments in aviation; and

- Safety Promotion in the form of engagement and discussion between both external stakeholders (e.g., the aviation training industry) and the FAA policy divisions going forward will determine the content of any ACS that publishes in a Notice of Proposed Rulemaking.

The FAA develops the ACS documents along with associated guidance and updated reference material in collaboration with a diverse group of aviation training experts. The goal is to drive a systematic approach to all components of the airman certification system, including knowledge test question development and conduct of the practical test. The FAA acknowledges and appreciates the many hours that these aviation experts have contributed toward this goal. This level of collaboration, a hallmark of a robust safety culture, strengthens and enhances aviation safety at every level of the airman certification system.

Note: This document does not apply to the Practical Test Standards.

The Non-Regulatory Material in this Guide

This guide provides test preparatory information for an applicant seeking a certificate or rating. This guide also provides a list of references and abbreviations/acronyms used in any ACS and a practical test checklist for use by an applicant. The material in this guide is non-regulatory and may contain terms such as should or may:

- Should indicates actions that are recommended, but not regulatory.
- May is used in a permissive sense to state authority or permission to do the act prescribed.

This document is not legally binding and will not be relied upon by the FAA as a basis for affirmative enforcement action or other administrative penalty. Conformity with the guidance is voluntary only and nonconformity will not affect rights and obligations under existing statutes and regulations.

Section 1: Knowledge Test Eligibility, Description, and Registration

Eligibility

For detailed airman knowledge test eligibility and applicable prerequisites, applicants should refer to the 14 CFR part 61 rules that apply to a specific certificate or rating.

Steps for Knowledge Test Registration

Step 1. Obtain an FAA Tracking Number

The FAA Airman Knowledge Test registration system requires the applicant to have an FAA Tracking Number (FTN). Applicants may obtain an FTN through the Integrated Airman Certification and Rating Application (IACRA) website.

This video describes creating an IACRA account and obtaining an FTN. The specific instructions begin at the 14-minute mark.

Step 2. Create an Account with PSI

After obtaining an FTN, applicants should create an account with the FAA's contracted testing vendor, PSI, a professional testing company which operates hundreds of test centers. Visit PSI's website for information on authorized airman knowledge test centers and how to register, schedule, and pay for an Airman Knowledge Test:

> **Note:** *The IACRA and PSI systems share data that verifies the applicant's FTN and name based on the information input into IACRA by the applicant. The PSI system does not allow applicants to make changes to their name. Applicants who need to make a correction to their name should process that correction in the IACRA system. The applicant's name correction will appear in the PSI system once the applicant logs back into the PSI system and refreshes their account.*

Step 3. Select Test and Testing Center

After obtaining an FTN and creating an account with PSI, applicants may schedule knowledge tests. The PSI system walks the applicant through the process to select a test center in their area and select one or more specific knowledge tests.

Step 4. Select an Available Time Slot

After selecting the test center and test, the applicant may select a date and time slot.

Step 5. Pay for Test

After selecting an available time slot, the PSI system prompts the applicant to pay for the test. After completing this step, the applicant receives an automated email confirmation from PSI.

Applicants are required to meet any applicable Airman Knowledge Test eligibility requirements before arriving at a test center to take a specific knowledge test.

Testing Procedures for Applicants Requesting Special Accommodations

Applicants may request a special accommodation for their airman knowledge test through the PSI test registration and scheduling process. The process allows the applicant to select the specific accommodation(s) needed in accordance with the Americans with Disabilities Act (ADA). The PSI special accommodations team will work with the applicant and the selected testing center to provide appropriate accommodation(s). The PSI special accommodations team may request medical documentation for verification.

Acceptable Forms of Identification

14 CFR part 61, section 61.35, requires an applicant for a knowledge test to have proper identification at the time of application. Before beginning an Airman Knowledge Test, test center personnel will ask to see the applicant's state or federal government-issued photo identification. The identification must contain the applicant's photograph, signature, and date of birth. If the applicant's permanent mailing address is a PO Box number, the applicant must provide a current residential address.

Acceptable Forms of Applicant Address Verification

The table below provides examples of acceptable identification.

All Applicants	U.S. Citizens & Resident Aliens	Non-U.S. Citizens
Identification information must be: ✓ valid ✓ current Identification must include **all** of the following information: ✓ photo ✓ date of birth ✓ signature ✓ physical, residential address	✓ Identification card issued by any **U.S.** state, territory, or government entity (e.g., driver permit or license, government identification card, or military identification card) **or** ✓ Passport **or** ✓ Alien residency card	✓ Passport **and** ✓ Driver permit or license issued by a U.S. state or territory **or** ✓ Identification card issued by any government entity

Airman Knowledge Test Description

The airman knowledge test consists of multiple-choice questions. A single correct response exists for each test question. A correct response to one question does not depend upon, or influence, the correct response to another.

Taking the Knowledge Test

Before starting the actual test, the test center provides an applicant with the opportunity to practice navigating the test software. This practice or tutorial session may include sample questions to familiarize the applicant with the look and feel of the software (e.g., selecting an answer, marking a question for later review, monitoring time remaining for the test, and other features of the testing software). PSI also provides sample tests for registered users on their website.

Acceptable and Unacceptable Materials

The applicant may use the following aids, reference materials, and test materials when taking the knowledge test provided the material does not include actual test questions or answers:

Acceptable Materials	Unacceptable Materials	Notes
Supplement book provided by the proctor	Written materials that are handwritten, printed, or electronic	Testing centers may provide calculators and/or deny the use of personal calculators.
All models of aviation-oriented calculators or small electronic calculators that perform only arithmetic functions	Electronic calculators incorporating permanent or continuous type memory circuits without erasure capability	Proctor may prohibit the use of an applicant's calculator if the proctor is unable to determine the calculator's erasure capability
Calculators with simple programmable memories, which allow the addition to, subtraction from, or retrieval of one number from the memory, or simple functions, such as square root and percentages	Magnetic Cards, magnetic tapes, modules, computer chips, or any other device upon which pre-written programs or information related to the test can be stored and retrieved	Printouts of data should be surrendered at the completion of the test if the calculator incorporates this design feature
Scales, straightedges, protractors, plotters, navigation computers, blank log sheets, holding pattern entry aids, and electronic or mechanical calculators that are directly related to the test	Dictionaries	Before, and upon completion of the test, while in the presence of the proctor, actuate the ON/OFF switch or RESET button, and perform any other function that ensures erasure of any data stored in memory circuits
Manufacturer's permanently inscribed instructions on the front and back of such aids (e.g., formulas, conversions, regulations, signals, weather data, holding pattern diagrams, frequencies, weight and balance formulas, and air traffic control procedures)	Any booklet or manual containing instructions related to the use of test aids	Proctor makes the final determination regarding aids, reference materials, and test materials

Test Taking Tips

When taking a knowledge test, applicants should:

- Read the test instructions carefully;
- Mark difficult questions for later review in order to use the available time efficiently;
- Examine graphs and notes that pertain to the question;
- Request and mark a printed copy of any graph while computing answers, if needed;
- Understand that since only one answer is complete and correct, the other possible answers are either incomplete or erroneous;
- Answer each question in accordance with the current regulations and guidance publications; and
- Answer all the questions before time allotted for the test expires.
- Review 14 CFR part 61, section 61.37 regarding cheating or other unauthorized conduct.

Section 2: Airman Knowledge Test Report

Upon completion of the knowledge test, the test center issues a printed Airman Knowledge Test Report (AKTR) to the applicant, which documents the applicant's test score and lists a code for any questions answered incorrectly. The applicant should retain the original AKTR. During the oral portion of a practical test, the evaluator reviews the AKTR, and assesses any noted areas of deficiency.

Applicant Name Considerations for the Airman Knowledge Test Report and the Practical Test

The FAA compares the applicant's name on the AKTR with the name on the practical test application form when examining certificate and rating applications and before issuing a permanent certificate to the applicant. If an incorrect middle initial, spelling variant, or different middle name is on the AKTR or if there is a first name variation of any kind between the AKTR and the formal application for a certificate or rating, the evaluator for the practical test should attach an explanation and a copy of the applicant's photo identification to the IACRA or paper application. An IACRA application cannot be processed if the applicant's last name or suffix (e.g., Jr., Sr.) on the AKTR does not match the name recorded on the application form. In this case, the applicant should use a paper application, and the evaluator should include an explanation and copy of the applicant's photo identification to avoid a correction notice.

Retesting After Failure of AKTR

An applicant retesting after the failure of any Airman Knowledge Test may retest with appropriate authorization. The applicant should bring the applicable AKTR indicating failure to the test center, along with an endorsement from an Authorized Instructor who gave the applicant the required additional training in accordance with 14 CFR part 61, section 61.49. The endorsement certifies that the applicant is competent to pass the knowledge test.

Knowledge Test Codes During Transition from PTS To ACS

When a PTS is the effective standard for a specific certificate or rating, the applicant receives an Airman Knowledge Test Report with pilot (PLT) codes that correspond to any knowledge test question(s) the applicant answered incorrectly. For example: PLT044.

For knowledge tests taken after an ACS becomes the effective standard for a specific certificate or rating, the test center issues an AKTR with ACS codes that correspond to any knowledge test question(s) the applicant answered incorrectly. For example: CA.I.A.K1

During a period of transition after an ACS replaces a PTS, an applicant could possess a valid AKTR with PLT codes. When this occurs, instructors and evaluators can continue to use PLT codes in conjunction with the appropriate ACS for targeting training and retesting of missed knowledge subject areas by looking up the PLT code(s) in the Learning Statement Reference Guide.

After noting the subject area(s) for the PLT codes, instructors and evaluators should check or test the applicant's understanding of that material in the context of the appropriate ACS Area(s) of Operation and Task(s).

> **Note:** *Test codes for the Fundamentals of Instructing knowledge test are the same for all instructor certificates and will issue with ACS codes after the first instructor ACS becomes effective.*

ACS Archived Test Codes

As a result of updates made to an ACS, an AKTR may contain one or more archived ACS codes. These codes are indicated as archived within the ACS. For example:

> PA.VIII.E.K1a   Archived.

Use of archived codes in the ACS avoids code shifting that could create ambiguity when looking up ACS codes listed on an AKTR. An unexpired AKTR may span ACS revisions and ACS codes may archive after an applicant takes a knowledge test. Therefore, an applicant, instructor, or evaluator may need to interpret one or more archived ACS codes on an AKTR. Individuals can refer to the ACS revision in effect on the date of the knowledge test or to section 8 of this guide for archived ACS codes and the associated element text.

Use of archived codes in the ACS avoids code shifting that could create ambiguity when looking up ACS codes listed on an AKTR. An unexpired AKTR may span ACS revisions and ACS codes may archive after an applicant takes a knowledge test. Therefore, an applicant, instructor, or evaluator may need to interpret one or more archived ACS codes on an AKTR. Individuals can refer to the ACS revision in effect on the date of the knowledge test or to Section 8 of this guide for archived ACS codes and the associated element text. For example, the archived ACS code for Private Pilot Airplane element PA.VIII.E.K1a is noted in Section 8 of this guide as: Sensitivity, limitations, and potential errors in unusual attitudes.

Obtaining a Duplicate AKTR

If the applicant's knowledge test was taken on or after January 13, 2020, the applicant can print a duplicate or expired test report (AKTR) by visiting the PSI website.

If the knowledge test was taken on or before January 10, 2020, the applicant should follow 14 CFR, section 61.29 for replacement of a lost or destroyed AKTR.

Section 3: ACS Risk Management

Risk management involves perception of hazards, the ability to process the probability and severity of outcomes associated with any hazard, and performance of appropriate risk mitigation as needed to preserve the desired margin of safety.

Previous editions of the ACS often used elements for evaluation of risk management as encompassing a failure to do something. Many of these "failure to act" elements mimicked skill elements and limited an evaluator's opportunity to thoroughly examine an applicant's understanding of risk management.

For example, see elements R1 and S2 from the Private Pilot — Airplane Airman Certification Standards (FAA-S-ACS-6B with Change 1) in the excerpt below:

Task	C. Systems and Equipment Malfunctions
References	FAA-H-8083-2, FAA-H-8083-3; POH/AFM
Objective	To determine that the applicant exhibits satisfactory knowledge, risk management, and skills associated with system and equipment malfunctions appropriate to the airplane provided for the practical test and analyzing the situation and take appropriate action for simulated emergencies.
Knowledge	The applicant demonstrates understanding of:
PA.IX.C.K1	Partial or complete power loss related to the specific powerplant, including:
PA.IX.C.K1a	a. Engine roughness or overheat
PA.IX.C.K1b	b. Carburetor or induction icing
PA.IX.C.K1c	c. Loss of oil pressure
PA.IX.C.K1d	d. Fuel starvation
PA.IX.C.K2	System and equipment malfunctions specific to the airplane, including:
PA.IX.C.K2a	a. Electrical malfunction
PA.IX.C.K2b	b. Vacuum/pressure and associated flight instrument malfunctions
PA.IX.C.K2c	c. Pitot/static system malfunction
PA.IX.C.K2d	d. Electronic flight deck display malfunction
PA.IX.C.K2e	e. Landing gear or flap malfunction
PA.IX.C.K2f	f. Inoperative trim
PA.IX.C.K3	Smoke/fire/engine compartment fire.
PA.IX.C.K4	Any other system specific to the airplane (e.g., supplemental oxygen, deicing).
PA.IX.C.K5	Inadvertent door or window opening.
Risk Management	The applicant demonstrates the ability to identify, assess and mitigate risks, encompassing:
PA.IX.C.R1	Failure to use the proper checklist for a system or equipment malfunction.
PA.IX.C.R2	Distractions, loss of situational awareness, or improper task management.
Skills	The applicant demonstrates the ability to:
PA.IX.C.S1	Describe appropriate action for simulated emergencies specified by the evaluator, from at least three of the elements or sub-elements listed in K1 through K5 above.
PA.IX.C.S2	Complete the appropriate checklist.

The FAA reworded risk elements that describe a Failure to... (or similar phrases) with language permitting an open-ended examination of risk management by the evaluator. See element R2 in the excerpt below (image for illustration purposes only):

Task C. Systems and Equipment Malfunctions

References: FAA-H-8083-2, FAA-H-8083-3, FAA-H-8083-25; POH/AFM

Objective: To determine the applicant exhibits satisfactory knowledge, risk management, and skills associated with system and equipment malfunctions appropriate to the airplane provided for the practical test.

Knowledge:	The applicant demonstrates understanding of:
PA.IX.C.K1	Causes of partial or complete power loss related to the specific type of powerplant(s).
PA.IX.C.K1a	a. [Archived]
PA.IX.C.K1b	b. [Archived]
PA.IX.C.K1c	c. [Archived]
PA.IX.C.K1d	d. [Archived]
PA.IX.C.K2	System and equipment malfunctions specific to the aircraft, including:
PA.IX.C.K2a	a. Electrical malfunction
PA.IX.C.K2b	b. Vacuum/pressure and associated flight instrument malfunctions
PA.IX.C.K2c	c. Pitot-static system malfunction
PA.IX.C.K2d	d. Electronic flight deck display malfunction
PA.IX.C.K2e	e. Landing gear or flap malfunction
PA.IX.C.K2f	f. Inoperative trim
PA.IX.C.K3	Causes and remedies for smoke or fire onboard the aircraft.
PA.IX.C.K4	Any other system specific to the aircraft (e.g., supplemental oxygen, deicing).
PA.IX.C.K5	Inadvertent door or window opening.

Risk Management:	The applicant is able to identify, assess, and mitigate risk associated with:
PA.IX.C.R1	Checklist usage for a system or equipment malfunction.
PA.IX.C.R2	Distractions, task prioritization, loss of situational awareness, or disorientation.
PA.IX.C.R3	Undesired aircraft state.
PA.IX.C.R4	Startle response.

Skills:	The applicant exhibits the skill to:
PA.IX.C.S1	Determine appropriate action for simulated emergencies specified by the evaluator, from at least three of the elements or sub-elements listed in K1 through K5.
PA.IX.C.S2	Complete the appropriate checklist(s).

Section 4: Flight Instructor Applicant Considerations

Flight Instructor ACS Information

Flight Instructor ACS documents include sections that define the acceptable standards for knowledge, risk management, and skills unique to an instructor certificate or rating.

Knowledge elements often begin with "The applicant demonstrates instructional knowledge by describing and explaining…" Instructional knowledge means the instructor applicant can effectively present the what, how, and why involved with the task elements using techniques described in the fundamentals of instructing (FOI) area of operation in an instructor ACS.

The Fundamentals of Instructing (FOI), Area of Operation I, Task F: Elements of Effective Teaching that include Risk Management and Accident Prevention focuses on teaching risk management and on those risks encountered by a flight instructor while providing in-flight instruction.

Instructor applicants deal with additional risk management on several levels. These include teaching risk management in the classroom and mitigation of risk during flight instruction.

Note that the FOI sections in each instructor ACS are identical and use the same element codes. This makes it possible to use the same FOI elements for every instructor ACS.

Section 5: References

The ACS are based on the following 14 CFR parts, FAA guidance documents, manufacturer's publications, and other documents.

Note: *Users should reference the current edition of the reference documents listed below. The current edition of all FAA publications can be found at www.faa.gov.*

Reference	Title
14 CFR part 1	Definitions and Abbreviations
14 CFR part 23	Airworthiness Standards: Normal Category Airplanes
14 CFR part 25	Airworthiness Standards: Transport Category Airplanes
14 CFR part 27	Airworthiness Standards: Normal Category Rotorcraft
14 CFR part 29	Airworthiness Standards: Transport Category Rotorcraft
14 CFR part 39	Airworthiness Directives
14 CFR part 43	Maintenance, Preventive Maintenance, Rebuilding, and Alteration
14 CFR part 61	Certification: Pilots, Flight Instructors, and Ground Instructors
14 CFR part 63	Certification: Flight Crewmembers other than Pilots
14 CFR part 65	Certification: Airmen Other Than Flightcrew Members
14 CFR part 67	Medical Standards and Certification
14 CFR part 68	Requirements for Operating Certain Small Aircraft Without a Medical Certificate
14 CFR part 71	Designation of Class A, B, C, D, and E Airspace Areas; Air Traffic Service Routes; and Reporting Points
14 CFR part 91	General Operating and Flight Rules
14 CFR part 93	Special Air Traffic Rules
14 CFR part 97	Standard Instrument Procedures
14 CFR part 117	Flight and Duty Limitations and Rest Requirements: Flightcrew Members
14 CFR part 119	Certification: Air Carriers and Commercial Operators
14 CFR part 121	Operating Requirements: Domestic, Flag, and Supplemental Operations
14 CFR part 135	Operating Requirements: Commuter and on Demand Operations and Rules Governing Persons on Board Such Aircraft
49 CFR part 830	Notification and Reporting of Aircraft Accidents or Incidents and Overdue Aircraft, and Preservation of Aircraft Wreckage, Mail, Cargo, and Records
AC 00-30	Clear Air Turbulence Avoidance
AC 00-46	Aviation Safety Reporting Program
AC 20-117	Hazards Following Ground Deicing and Ground Operations in Conditions Conducive to Aircraft Icing
AC 29-2	Certification of Transport Category Rotorcraft
AC 60-22	Aeronautical Decision Making
AC 60-28	FAA English Language Standard for an FAA Certificate Issued Under 14 CFR Parts 61, 63, 65, and 107
AC 61-65	Certification: Pilots and Flight and Ground Instructors

Reference	Title
AC 61-67	Stall and Spin Awareness Training
AC 61-107	Aircraft Operations at Altitudes Above 25,000 Feet Mean Sea Level or Mach Numbers Greater Than .75
AC 61-138	Airline Transport Pilot Certification Training Program
AC 61-140	Autorotation Training
AC 68-1	BasicMed
AC 90-48	Pilots' Role in Collision Avoidance
AC 90-95	Unanticipated Right Yaw in Helicopters
AC 90-100	U.S Terminal and En Route Area Navigation (RNAV) Operations
AC 90-105	Approval Guidance for RNP Operations and Barometric Vertical Navigation in the U.S. National Airspace System and in Oceanic and Remote Continental Airspace
AC 90-107	Guidance for Localizer Performance with Vertical Guidance and Localizer Performance without Vertical Guidance Approach Operations in the U.S. National Airspace System
AC 90-117	Data Link Communications
AC 91.21-1	Use of Portable Electronic Devices Aboard Aircraft
AC 91-32	Safety in and Around Helicopters
AC 91-55	Reduction of Electrical System Failures Following Aircraft Engine Starting
AC 91-73	Parts 91 and 135 Single Pilot, Flight School Procedures During Taxi Operations
AC 91-74	Pilot Guide: Flight in Icing Conditions
AC 91-78	Use of Class 1 or Class 2 Electronic Flight Bag (EFB)
AC 91-79	Mitigating the Risks of a Runway Overrun Upon Landing
AC 91-92	Pilot's Guide to a Preflight Briefing
AC 120-27	Aircraft Weight and Balance Control
AC 120-51	Crew Resource Management Training
AC 120-57	Surface Movement Guidance and Control System
AC 120-58	Pilot Guide Large Aircraft Ground Deicing
AC 120-60	Ground Deicing and Anti-icing Program
AC 120-66	Aviation Safety Action Program (ASAP)
AC 120-71	Standard Operating Procedures and Pilot Monitoring Duties for Flight Deck Crewmembers
AC 120-74	Parts 91, 121, 125, and 135 Flightcrew Procedures During Taxi Operations
AC 120-76	Authorization for Use of Electronic Flight Bags
AC 120-82	Flight Operational Quality Assurance (FOQA)
AC 120-90	Line Operations Safety Audit (LOSA)
AC 120-100	Basics of Aviation Fatigue
AC 120-101	Part 121 Air Carrier Operational Control
AC 120-108	Continuous Descent Final Approach

Reference	Title
AC 120-109	Stall Prevention and Recovery Training
AC 120-111	Upset Prevention and Recovery Training
AC 135-17	Pilot Guide - Small Aircraft Ground Deicing
AFM	Airplane Flight Manual
AIM	Aeronautical Information Manual
AC 120-100	Basics of Aviation Fatigue
AC 120-101	Part 121 Air Carrier Operational Control
AC 120-108	Continuous Descent Final Approach
AC 120-109	Stall Prevention and Recovery Training
AC 120-111	Upset Prevention and Recovery Training
AC 135-17	Pilot Guide - Small Aircraft Ground Deicing
AFM	Airplane Flight Manual
AIM	Aeronautical Information Manual
Applicable Manufacturer's Equipment Supplement(s)	Manufacturer's Equipment Supplement(s)
Appropriate Manufacturer's Safety Notices	Safety Notices
Chart Supplements	Chart Supplements
Digital-Visual Charts (d-VC)	Digital-Visual Charts (d-VC)
FAA-H-8083-1	Aircraft Weight and Balance Handbook
FAA-H-8083-2	Risk Management Handbook
FAA-H-8083-3	Airplane Flying Handbook
FAA-H-8083-9	Aviation Instructor's Handbook
FAA-H-8083-15	Instrument Flying Handbook
FAA-H-8083-16	Instrument Procedures Handbook
FAA-H-8083-21	Helicopter Flying Handbook
FAA-H-8083-23	Seaplane, Skiplane, and Float/Ski Equipped Helicopter Operations Handbook
FAA-H-8083-25	Pilot's Handbook of Aeronautical Knowledge
FAA-H-8083-28	Aviation Weather Handbook
FAA Order 8130.2	Airworthiness Certification of Aircraft
FAA-P-8740-66	Flying Light Twins Safely
FSB Report (type specific)	Flight Standardization Board Report (if available)
Helicopter Route Charts	Helicopter Route Charts
IFR Enroute Charts	IFR Enroute Low Altitude and IFR Enroute High Altitude Charts
NOTAMs	Notices to Air Missions
PDC	Profile Descent Charts

Reference	Title
POH/AFM	Pilot's Operating Handbook/FAA-Approved Airplane Flight Manual
POH/Flight Manual	Pilot's Operating Handbook/FAA-Approved Flight Manual
POH/RFM	Pilot's Operating Handbook/FAA-Approved Rotorcraft Flight Manual
QRH	Quick Reference Handbook
SAFO 16016	Helicopter Stabilized Hover Checks Before Departure
SAFO 17010	Incorrect Airport Surface Approaches and Landings
SAFO 19001	Landing Performance Assessments at Time of Arrival
STARs	Standard Terminal Arrival Routes
TPP	Terminal Procedures Publications
USCG Navigation Rules	USCG Navigation Rules, International-Inland
VFR Navigation Charts	Sectional/Terminal Aeronautical Charts

Section 6: Abbreviations and Acronyms

Note: *Users should reference the current edition of the reference documents listed below. The current edition of all FAA publications can be found at www.faa.gov.*

Acronym	Description
14 CFR	Title 14 of the Code of Federal Regulations
AATD	Advanced Aviation Training Device
AC	Advisory Circular
ACS	Airman Certification Standards
ADM	Aeronautical Decision-Making
ADS-B	Automatic Dependent Surveillance Broadcast
ADS-C	Automatic Dependent Surveillance - Contract
AFCS	Automatic Flight Control System
AFM	Airplane Flight Manual
AGL	Above Ground Level
AIM	Aeronautical Information Manual
AIRMET	Airman's Meteorological Information
AKTR	Airman Knowledge Test Report
AMEL	Airplane Multiengine Land
AMES	Airplane Multiengine Sea
APU	Auxiliary Power Unit
ASEL	Airplane Single-Engine Land
ASES	Airplane Single-Engine Sea
ASI	Aviation Safety Inspector
ATC	Air Traffic Control
ATD	Aviation Training Device
ATP	Airline Transport Pilot
BATD	Basic Aviation Training Device
CDI	Course Deviation Indicator
CDL	Configuration Deviation List
CFIT	Controlled Flight Into Terrain
CFR	Code of Federal Regulations
CG	Center of Gravity
CPDLC	Controller–pilot data link communication
CRM	Crew Resource Management
DA	Decision Altitude
DDA	Derived Decision Altitude

ACS Companion Guide for Pilots (FAA-G-ACS-2)

Acronym	Description
DH	Decision Height
DME	Distance Measuring Equipment
DP	Departure Procedures
EFB	Electronic Flight Bag
EFC	Expect Further Clearance
EFIS	Electronic Flight Instrument System
ELT	Emergency Locator Transmitter
ETA	Estimated Time of Arrival
ETL	Effective Translational Lift
FAA	Federal Aviation Administration
FAF	Final Approach Fix
FB	Wind and Temperature Aloft Forecast
FFS	Full Flight Simulator
FMS	Flight Management System
FRAT	Flight Risk Assessment Tool
FSB	Flight Standardization Board
FSO	Flight Standards Office
FSTD	Flight Simulation Training Device
FTD	Flight Training Device
G	Unit of Force Equal to Earth's Gravity
GBAS	Ground Based Augmentation System
GFA	Graphical Forecast for Aviation
GNSS	Global Navigation Satellite System
GPS	Global Positioning System
H/V	Height/Velocity
HF	High Frequency
HIGE	Hover In Ground Effect
HUD	Head Up Display
IFR	Instrument Flight Rules
ILS	Instrument Landing System
IMC	Instrument Meteorological Conditions
INFO	Information for Operators
INS	Inertial Navigation System
IOS	Instructor Operating Station
KOEL	Kinds of Operations Equipment List
L/DMAX	Lift/Drag Maximum

Acronym	Description
LAHSO	Land and Hold Short Operations
LNAV	Lateral Navigation
LOA	Letter of Authorization
LOC-I	Loss of Control in Flight
LP	Localizer Performance
LTE	Loss of Tail Rotor Effectiveness
LTM	Long Term Memory
MAP	Missed Approach Point
MDA	Minimum Descent Altitude
MEL	Minimum Equipment List
METAR	Aviation Routine Weather Reports (Meteorological Aerodrome Report)
MFD	Multi-Function Display
MMO	Maximum Operating Limit Speed as a Mach Number
NAS	National Airspace System
NOTAM	Notice to Air Missions
Nr	Main Rotor Speed
NSP	National Simulator Program
NTSB	National Transportation Safety Board
ODP	Obstacle Departure Procedure
OEI	One Engine Inoperative
PAVE	Risk Management Checklist for Pilot/Aircraft/enVironment/External Factors
PFD	Primary Flight Display
PIC	Pilot-in-Command
PinS	Copter Point in Space
PIREP	Pilot Report
POA	Plan of Action
POH	Pilot's Operating Handbook
PTS	Practical Test Standards
QPS	Qualification Performance Standard
QRH	Quick Reference Handbook
RAIM	Receiver Autonomous Integrity Monitoring
RCAM	Runway Condition Assessment Matrix
RFM	Rotorcraft Flight Manual
RNAV	Area Navigation
RNP	Required Navigation Performance
RPM	Revolutions Per Minute

Acronym	Description
SAE	Specialty Aircraft Examiner
SAFO	Safety Alert for Operators
SATR	Special Air Traffic Rules
SBAS	Satellite Based Augmentation System
SBT	Scenario Based Training
SFAR	Special Federal Aviation Regulation
SFRA	Special Flight Rules Area
SID	Standard Instrument Departure
SIGMET	Significant Meteorological Information
SMS	Safety Management System
SRM	Single-Pilot Resource Management
SRM	Safety Risk Management
STAR	Standard Terminal Arrival
STM	Short Term Memory
SUA	Special Use Airspace
TAF	Terminal Area Forecast
TAWS	Terrain Awareness and Warning System
TCAS	Traffic Collision Avoidance System
TCDS	Type Certificate Data Sheet
TCE	Training Center Evaluator
TEM	Threat and Error Management
TFR	Temporary Flight Restrictions
TPP	Terminal Procedures Publication
TUC	Time of Useful Consciousness
UHF	Ultra High Frequency
UIMC	Unintended Instrument Meteorological Conditions
USCG	United States Coast Guard
UTC	Coordinated Universal Time
V_1	The maximum speed in the takeoff at which the pilot must take the first action (e.g., apply brakes, reduce thrust, deploy speed brakes) to stop the airplane within the accelerate-stop distance. V_1 also means the minimum speed in the takeoff, following a failure of the critical engine at V_{EF}, at which the pilot can continue the takeoff and achieve the required height above the takeoff surface within the takeoff distance.
V_2	Takeoff Safety Speed
V_A	Maneuvering speed
VDP	Visual Descent Point
VFR	Visual Flight Rules

Acronym	Description
V_{MC}	Minimum control speed with the critical engine inoperative
VHF	Very High Frequency
VMC	Visual Meteorological Conditions
V_{MCG}	Minimum control speed on the ground with the critical engine inoperative
V_{MO}	Maximum Operating Limit Speed
V_{NE}	Never exceed speed
VCOA	Visual Climb Over Airport
VOR	Very High Frequency Omnidirectional Range
V_R	Rotation speed
V_{REF}	Reference Landing Speed
VRS	Vortex Ring State
V_S	Stall Speed
V_{SO}	Stalling Speed or the Minimum Steady Flight Speed in the Landing Configuration
V_{SSE}	Safe, intentional one-engine-inoperative speed. Originally known as safe single-engine speed
VTOL	Vertical Takeoff and Landing
V_X	Best angle of climb airspeed
V_{XSE}	Best angle of climb speed with one engine inoperative
V_Y	Best rate of climb speed
V_{YSE}	Best rate of climb speed with one engine inoperative.
WAAS	Wide Area Augmentation System

ACS Companion Guide for Pilots (FAA-G-ACS-2)

Section 7: Practical Test Checklist (Applicant)

Evaluator's Name: _____

Location: _____

Date/Time: _____

Acceptable Aircraft

- ☐ Aircraft Documents:
  - ☐ Airworthiness Certificate
  - ☐ Registration Certificate
  - ☐ Operating Limitations
- ☐ Aircraft Maintenance Records:
  - ☐ Logbook Record of Airworthiness Inspections and Airworthiness Directives (AD) Compliance
- ☐ Pilot's Operating Handbook and FAA-Approved Aircraft Flight Manual

Personal Equipment

- ☐ View-Limiting Device
- ☐ Current Aeronautical Charts (printed or electronic)
- ☐ Computer and Plotter
- ☐ Flight Plan Form and Flight Logs (printed or electronic)
- ☐ Chart Supplements, Airport Diagrams, and Appropriate Publications (printed or electronic)
- ☐ Current AIM (printed or electronic)

Personal Records

- ☐ Government-Issued Identification—Photo/Signature Identification (ID)
- ☐ Pilot Certificate
- ☐ Current Medical Certificate or BasicMed Qualification (when applicable)
- ☐ Completed FAA Form 8710-1, Airman Certificate and/or Rating Application, or completed IACRA form, FAA Form 8710-11, Airman Certificate and/or Rating Application—Sport Pilot, or FAA Form 8400.3, Airman Certificate and/or Rating Application with Instructor's Signature, if applicable
- ☐ Airman Knowledge Test Report
- ☐ Airman's Logbook with Appropriate Instructor Endorsements
- ☐ FAA Form 8060-5, Notice of Disapproval (if applicable)
- ☐ Letter of Discontinuance (if applicable)
- ☐ Approved School Graduation Certificate (if applicable)

Section 8: Knowledge Test Reports and Archived ACS Codes

Private Pilot for Airplane Category ACS Archived Codes

PA.III.A.R3	Confirmation or expectation bias.
PA.IV.A.S10	Retract the water rudders, as appropriate, establish and maintain the most efficient planing/liftoff attitude, and correct for porpoising and skipping (ASES, AMES).
PA.IV.I.S5	Retract the water rudders as appropriate; advance the throttle smoothly to takeoff power.
PA.IV.K.S7	Retract the water rudders as appropriate; advance the throttle smoothly to takeoff power.
PA.VIII.E.K1a	Sensitivity, limitations, and potential errors in unusual attitudes
PA.VIII.E.K1b	Correlation (pitch instruments/bank instruments)
PA.VIII.E.K1c	Function and operation
PA.VIII.E.K1d	Proper instrument cross-check techniques
PA.VIII.E.R2	Failure to seek assistance or declare an emergency in a deteriorating situation.
PA.VIII.E.R6	Failure to unload the wings in recovering from high G situations.
PA.VIII.F.S3	Maintain altitude ±200 feet, heading ±20°, and airspeed ±10 knots.
PA.IX.C.K1a	Maintain altitude ±200 feet, heading ±20°, and airspeed ±10 knots
PA.IX.C.K1b	Engine roughness or overheat
PA.IX.C.K1c	Loss of oil pressure
PA.IX.C.K1d	Fuel starvation
PA.XII.A.R2	Confirmation or expectation bias as related to taxi instructions.
PA.XII.A.S1	Demonstrate runway incursion avoidance procedures.
PA.XII.B.R2	Confirmation or expectation bias as related to taxi instructions.

Commercial Pilot for Airplane Category ACS Archived Codes

CA.I.F.K2f   Weight and balance

CA.IV.A.S10   Retract the water rudders, as appropriate, establish and maintain the most efficient planing/liftoff attitude, and correct for porpoising and skipping (ASES, AMES).

CA.IV.I.S5   Retract the water rudders as appropriate; advance the throttle smoothly to takeoff power.

CA.IV.K.S7   Retract the water rudders as appropriate; advance the throttle smoothly to takeoff power.

CA.IV.B.S5   Recognize signal loss or interference and take appropriate action, if applicable.

CA.IX.C.K1a   Engine roughness or overheat

CA.IX.C.K1b   Carburetor or induction icing

CA.IX.C.K1c   Loss of oil pressure

CA.IX.C.K1d   Fuel starvation

CA.XI.A.R2   Confirmation or expectation bias as related to taxi instructions.

CA.XI.A.S1   Utilize runway incursion avoidance procedures.

CA.XI.B.R2   Confirmation or expectation bias as related to taxi instructions.

Instrument Rating – Airplane ACS Archived Codes

IR.IV.B.R2   Failure to recognize an unusual flight attitude and follow the proper recovery procedure.

IR.VII.C.R2   Collision hazards, to include aircraft, terrain, obstacles, wires, vehicles, vessels, persons, and wildlife.

Airline Transport Pilot and Type Rating ACS Archived Codes

AA.IV.B.R2   Failure to recognize an unusual flight attitude and follow the proper recovery procedure.

AA.V.A.S2   When accomplished in an FSTD, the entry should be consistent with the expected operational environment for a stall on takeoff or while on approach in a partial flap configuration with no minimum entry altitude defined.

AA.V.B.S2   When accomplished in an FSTD, the entry should be consistent with the expected operational environment for a stall in cruise flight with no minimum entry altitude defined.

AA.V.C.S2   When accomplished in an FSTD, the entry should be consistent with the expected operational environment for a stall when fully configured for landing with no minimum entry altitude defined.

AA.VI.F.R3   Planning for.

AA.VI.F.R3a   a. Missed Approach

AA.VI.F.R3b   b. Land and hold short operations (LAHSO)

AA.VI.H.R3   Planning for.

AA.VI.H.R3a   a. Missed Approach

AA.VI.H.R3b   b. Land and hold short operations (LAHSO)

AA.VIII.A.R2   Confirmation or expectation bias as related to taxi instructions.

AA.VIII.B.R2   Confirmation or expectation bias as related to taxi instructions.

[end of document]